# Time to Die

## Based on a true story

# Stan Wald

# PROLOGUE

**THE RIDE BEGINS**
September 16, 1961
9:00 PM

ANGRY CLOUDS ABOVE the western fringe of Los Angeles opened like a spigot.

The sudden volley pelted the two boys as they darted across the street, sloshing toward the safety of the Chevron station.

Protected from the deluge under the canopy, they shook off the rainwater from their bomber jackets like a dog shedding water. Soon, they began to haggle over which one had to go back out in the storm and hitchhike.

After some heated bickering, they agreed to settle the dilemma the old-fashioned way; by flipping a coin.

Rick dug a quarter from his change pocket and tossed it high in the air.

"Call it! And don't wait until it hits the ground like you usually do."

"Tails never fails, baby!" Steve shouted amid the overhead clatter, anxiously

1

watching the coin as it bounced atop the
slick concrete and rolled in a wide arc
before flattening with the perched eagle
face up.

"Hah! Like I always say, tails never
fails," he gloated while pulling out a small
black comb to reshape his ducktail.

Raking his hair in place, he cast a
glance at his scowling cohort.

"I see the look on your face," he said
with a sly grin. "You're pissed I won the
toss, aren't you? Seems like someone forgot
who got us a ride in an Eldorado, eh shmuck?
And a tricked-out one to boot!"

Rick clenched his jaw - he remembered
all too well what happened in the Caddy.
Without a word, he scooped up the quarter
that failed him and stepped into the
downpour.


WITH AN EYE on his best friend, Steve
relaxed against a support pillar and fired
up a Marlboro with his trusty Zippo. Drawing
in a lungful, he French-inhaled and allowed
his mind to drift.

The image of his girlfriend soon
filtered into his thoughts, slow dancing
with her in the bedroom. Fused as one, their
bodies moved in sync to Rosie and the
Originals singing "Angel Baby" on the hi-fi;

Sue whispering in his ear, *"When you are near me, my heart skips a beat. I can hardly stand on my own two feet...."*

The pleasant vision slowly ebbed, leaving him to wonder how the evening might have turned out if he hadn't bolted from her house in a fit of rage when she reneged on her promise - a vow to surrender to his pent-up desires with a night he would never forget.

Lost in the memory of what could have been, cold water seeping through a gap in the aluminum awning plopped on his head, snapping him back to the present; a Saturday night that began with high expectations, only to turn ugly.

Through the flurry of glistening rainfall, he forced his attention to the darkened storefronts along Robertson Boulevard; a vast array of low-profile commercial buildings constructed in the 30s and 40s.

Lining the main artery like San Francisco row houses, most of the cluttered shops maintained their original façades, adding to the nostalgic character of the old neighborhood.

On Saturdays, weary store owners shut their doors at dusk. By nine, the street appeared deserted and one of the only merchants open for business was the Chevron.

On rainy nights, its glaring floodlights stood out like a watchtower, reflecting distorted images off the shimmering roadway.

Bored, Steve peered over his shoulder at the historical boundary marker no more than fifty feet away: WELCOME TO BEVERLY HILLS.

With a twinge of envy, he stared at the sign thinking: the city where the rich and famous lived, all in elaborate mansions with assorted palm trees and manicured lawns the size of football fields nestled behind protective walls with ornate security gates - notable celebrities, film directors, producers, power brokers and high-ranking studio hacks; they all played in this prestigious and pretentious Land of Oz, where life appeared idyllic.

*One day I'm going live there when I'm a well-known actor*, he reminded himself, then he turned and glimpsed once more at his pal cowering from the unrelenting assault, trying to flag down the occasional motorist.

From afar, he looked smaller, almost puny against the backdrop of water roiling feverishly off the asphalt.

**\*\*\*\***

IN TRUTH, both boys were considered short for their age. Wiry and well-proportioned, not an ounce of body fat on them, fourteen-year-old Rick stood five-foot four, and Steve, a year older, claimed to be two inches taller. Other than similarities in stature, they bore little else in common.

Rick Shoeman's bright hazel eyes complemented a slightly rounded face peppered with freckles and a bulbous nose destined to grow over the years. His mass of curly chestnut-brown hair was cropped close on the sides and neatly buzzed at the nape.

To those who knew him, he personified the typical boy-next-door; often labeled as average-looking but filled with unbridled zest and a warped sense of humor. His nerdy ways, however, were a stark contrast to his constant sidekick who projected a street-savvy arrogance.

Steve Bell did not conform to any societal modality, fashioning himself with the rebellious panache of James Dean as portrayed in *Rebel Without a Cause*. Much like the iconic star, he preferred wearing white tees with rolled-up sleeves and well-worn Levis riding low on the hips.

His lush dark-brown pompadour was styled straight back except for a clump of hair pulled forward in a cascading jellyroll. With a strong jawline and welcoming caramel-brown eyes, he made most teenyboppers melt. Many were quick to describe his unblemished baby-face as cute, a descriptive he loathed. To him, the word imparted femininity, something his macho-driven ego refused to tolerate.

**★★★★**

POWERFUL WIND GUSTS shifted the torrent to cascade in diagonal sheets, forcing Rick to shield his face from the painful slivers pricking at him like a thousand needles.

In the distance, he spotted the glow of high beams bearing down on him. Hunched over and squinting, he put his thumb in the air hoping to be seen, praying someone would pull over.

The headlamps abruptly disappeared, and as the blacked-out vehicle closed in, it slowed to a crawl before passing without stopping.

Perturbed at the ploy, Rick ran into the empty traffic lane gesturing with his middle finger, shouting obscenities as the car plowed through the overflowing interchange.

A corner of Steve's mouth rose. *He's such a putz. He'll be lucky if he makes it to eighteen.*

Minutes later another set of beams caught Rick's eye. He pumped his arm repeatedly until the black '57 Chevrolet Bel Air coasted to a stop in front of him.

A sense of déjà vu swept through him as he stared at the car - it resembled the one he flipped off moments ago, but in haste, he dismissed the notion and yanked on the door handle.

Never one to be fearful, he leaned inside, and as he did, water from his mop of hair dribbled onto the custom tuck-and-roll upholstery.

The handsome young man behind the wheel bared his teeth, then his dour expression seamlessly morphed into a strained smile: "Y'all need a lift?"

Eager for relief from the onslaught outside, Rick said, "You betcha!" and backed out, yelling over his shoulder toward the gas pumps: "C'mon boy, we've got a ride. Move it!"

With his coat pulled over his head, Steve dashed to the street helter-skelter in a hail of raindrops. Mid-way, he heard his friend holler, "Shotgun!"

"You're such an asshole," Steve hissed as he got within earshot, upset for missing the opportunity to sit in the prime seat. Miffed, he brushed past him and opened the door.

The startled driver hesitated before flashing a toothy smile: "Well hello there. My name's Loren ... and welcome to my web."

Taken aback by the odd remark, Steve scrunched his brow suspiciously and quickly sized him up: chiseled features like a handsome matinee idol, powerfully built and exceptionally tall, early twenties with tousled strawberry blond hair and lobeless ears flaring bat-like. Most noticeable were his crystal-blue eyes - the reflection from the dome-light made them appear translucent one moment, piercingly blue the next.

*Don't go!* warned a voice in his head, but the chilling rain and desire to hurry home outweighed the risk.

After a cursory glimpse at the rear compartment, he grabbed the backrest and pulled it forward to climb in.

"Hey kid, get out of there!" the man blurted, and patted the seat next to him. "You gotta sit up here because I got stuff in the back I don't want disturbed."

Steve cringed - three guys sitting leg-to-leg was not cool, especially sandwiched in between.

"What's the holdup?" Rick complained from behind.

Half out of the car, Steve repeated what the guy said.

"Get you sorry ass in because I'm getting soaked! We aren't going far so don't make it a big deal, okay?"

"All right! All right!" But now you owe
me two favors, he was about to say before
Rick shoved him inside, headfirst.


THE CHEVY EASED from the curb and
crossed Olympic when the light turned green.

As they navigated the flooded
thoroughfare, Steve noticed they were only
doing twenty in a forty mile-per-hour zone
and thought the man seemed extremely
pensive; not about the road or weather, but
something else.

He pulled his gaze from the gauge
cluster and eyed a foot-wide strip of two-
by-four mounted to the dashboard in front of
the passenger seat.

*How the hell did I miss that?* he
wondered, and nudged his buddy, motioning
with his head toward the oddity.

Glancing at the wood block, Rick
shrugged and shot him a comical, *I don't
know what the fuck it is either look.*

Their journey south continued in eerie
silence; not a word spoken. For Steve, each
uncomfortable minute felt like an hour.

From out of the blue, the driver began
chanting aloud, babbling garbled gibberish

in a sing-song fashion.

Wide-eyed, Steve turned to Rick, who was staring out the side window trying not to laugh.

Soon, the mantra ceased and the only sounds inside the car were that of heavy drops splattering against the windshield as the wipers beat their melodic tune akin to a huge metronome: *Swoosh ...swoosh ... swoosh.*

With the heater running full blast, the temperature inside had become excessively warm, and Steve detected the faint tang of body odor - it reminded him of the funky scent emitted when a person was nervous. His nostrils flared in protest at the sour metallic smell.

Every so often the man glanced in his direction as though conducting an inspection, then his eyes would dart away like a hummingbird.

It didn't take long before the tension became palpable, almost stifling.

Steve saw the same concern etched on Rick's face and pondered what to do next? His sixth sense screamed, *Get the fuck out. Now!*

Taking heed from his inner voice, as they approached the red stoplight, he said, "Mister, you can drop us off here instead of

Airdrome."

As if reading his mind, Rick chimed in. "Yeah, right. We need to stop at the grocery store," he said hastily, pointing to the Mayfair Market. "I've got buy a pack of smokes before going home."

Eyes agog, the man glared menacingly at Rick, then blinked several times as though awakened from a dream.

"No problem, boys. I'll let you off on the other side of the road where it's safer."

The light changed and they drove toward an unlit area where two overhead streetlamps had long burned out. The Chevy glided curbside seventy-five feet past the intersection and gradually came to rest.

BANG!

A loud crack suddenly echoed through the interior, and Rick screamed out, "Owwww! My back! I think I've been shot."

# CHAPTER 1

*PROJECT LIST*

1.   X̲   Rental House
2.   X̲   Gun / Ammo
3.   X̲   Cosmetic Case
4.   X̲   Switchblade
5.   X̲   Handcuffs
6.   X̲   Blankets / Towels
7.   X̲   Duct Tape
8.   X̲   Cement (nine bags)
9.   X̲   Chicken Wire (4 rolls)
10.  X̲   Water Jugs
11.  X̲   Heavy Duty Vise-grips
12.  X̲   Flashlight / Batteries
13.  X̲   Metal Strapping
14.  X̲   3/4" Threaded Pipe
15.  X̲   Bike Handbrake / Cable
16.  X̲   2x4x12 Wood Block
17.  X̲   Window / Door Handles
18.  X̲   Vaseline
19.  __   Duffel Bags (2)
20.  __   Burial Site
21.  __   Meat Saw

HUNCHED OVER THE dining room table, twenty-three-year-old Loren Neestrom carefully reviewed his *Project List*.

Scanning the dog-eared legal-size sheet line-by-line, he paused at *Item 21*. His tapered finger brushed over the number several times, and a corner of his mouth rose ever so slightly - the visual of two unsuspecting boys trapped inside his car popped into his thoughts. *They'll never suspect what's in store for them*, he mused.

The list was the first of thirty pages inside the faded-blue three-ring binder. The remaining twenty-nine detailed aspects of his treatise, a scheme conceived at eighteen, and by the time he turned twenty-one, it was typed into written form.

Although it had taken him years of meticulous preparation, the mounting anticipation of executing the plan taxed his patience with increased regularity, especially when dealing with his freaky mother.

"So very sexy," he whispered, perplexed how a natural beauty could be so diabolically wicked. "Thanks for passing along your fucked-up genes, bitch."

After closing the folder, he focused his attention on the set of hand-drawn blueprints he created while at work.

Unrolling one of the unwieldy thirty-six by twenty-four-inch faded sheets, he spread it over the grey Formica tabletop in the kitchen of his modest three-bedroom apartment he shared with his mother, Eleanor Neestrom, and nana, Annie Shanks.

Their rundown colonial-style fourplex on Juanita Place was in the seedier section of Hollywood's eastern fringe, well removed from the glitz and glamour associated with the entertainment capital of the world.

The whoosh from behind caught him off guard.

WHACK!

"You looking at naked girls again?" his mother bellowed while delivering a vicious knuckle-rap to his head.

Her pale-blue eyes widened with madness: "How many times do I have to tell you? They're pure evil; nothing but a bunch of filthy sluts to poison your mind and take you from me!"

Exceptionally attractive at forty-three, most people never saw Eleanor's dark side, a woman with a penchant for sadistic perversion and an insatiable libido from a scarred childhood.

Or the part that surfaced when she failed to take her doses of Thorazine and

14

miscellaneous psychotropic drugs. During those lapses, her rants would escalate for no reason and she'd scream at Loren with ear-piercing shrieks, distorting her angelic face. At times, her entire body would twitch while she made brushing motions with her hands down the sides of her legs as if warding off some imaginary creature assailing her torso.

Slowly, Loren turned away in a feeble attempt to fight back the nefarious hold she had on him and lowered his eyes in submission. Even though he towered over her petite frame, he always cringed under her icy gaze and caustic voice.

With his head bowed like a passive dog, he flashed back to the only time he had mustered the courage to escape her psychological grip....

**** 

A WEEK AFTER his eighteenth birthday, Loren and his mother and grandmother were at the table having their usual Friday night dinner of fish and chips.

In a hurry to catch an episode of Rawhide, one of his favorite television shows starring hunky Clint Eastwood, he hurriedly gobbled down his food and excused himself.

All through supper he observed his

mother's stilted body language, sensing she was on the verge of exploding with a drunken tirade.

Proving his instincts right, her piercing voice soon cut through the air, drowning out Rowdy Yates during a tense gunfight scene.

From what he overheard, the outburst was directed at nana - quite often Eleanor would lash out and blame Annie for unthinkable things that occurred to her as a precocious adolescent ... things involving her depraved father.

Irritated by the disruption, Loren hauled his hulk off the tattered sofa and marched into the kitchen, only to witness an attack on the one person he genuinely cared about - everyone else in his life meant nothing, superfluous objects to be used or abused.

He spotted his grandmother clutching a lace handkerchief in her withered hands while tears cascaded down her cheeks.

More than he could bear, his face flushed as he watched her being emotionally ripped apart.

A sudden rage surged through him when several of his malevolent alter-egos howled in unison: *KILL MOTHER! SMASH HER FACE IN!*

Out-of-control, he lunged at Eleanor, catching her by the throat.

Filled with pent-up hatred from a lifetime of physical exploitation, he slammed her against the wall and squeezed her neck with one hand while effortlessly hoisting her off the ground so they were face-to-face.

With his mouth mere inches from hers, their lips almost touching: "You ungrateful twat! Don't you ever talk to grandma like that again. Do you understand, Moth-er?" he screamed, showering her with spittle. "You're insane and need to go back to Camarillo, you crazy bitch!"

Eleanor's face turned a mottled shade of purple and her legs twitched like a dangling marionette.

"I wish you were dead," he hissed. "Look what you did to her! And think about all those things you've done to me."

His grasp tightened and the veins in his forearm bulged.

In desperation, Eleanor grasped the weighty cast iron pan from the wall bracket and clubbed him viciously across his head and shoulder.

The spurt of warm blood streaming down Loren's brow interrupted his frenzy and he released his hold, staring at her dispassionately as she crumpled to the worn linoleum in a heap, gasping for air.

The sound of Annie's hysterical cries soon replaced the cacophony assaulting his thoughts, and after regaining control of his senses, he spun around and lumbered down the long hallway, leaving behind a trail of crimson beads.

In the bathroom, a stream of blood dripped from his nose onto the ceramic tile floor, transforming the thin grooves of white grout into gutters of red.

Ignoring the mess, he stripped off his stained tee-shirt and dipped his head in the cracked porcelain bowl. After turning on the faucet, the water turned coppery-pink as it emptied into the drain.

Blindly, he plucked the bath-towel from the doorknob and wiped his face, then wrapped it around his head like a turban.

Loren glanced at himself in the mirror and almost burst out laughing - the tops of his shoulders were marred with welts; the largest reflecting the partial imprint of the letters, *L-O-D-G-E*, the name of the manufacturer embossed on the underside of the skillet.

*The cunt whacked me real good. I'll give her that.*

Moving in for a closer look, the knot of the towel unraveled, revealing a sizable gash oozing blood high on his forehead.

He knew just what to do, and grabbed the styptic pencil from his shaving kit, then wet the tapered end and placed the tip against the open wound.

The pain was intense, and his face screwed up like a clenched fist.

Once the bleeding subsided to a mere trickle, he rummaged through the cluttered medicine cabinet for a vial of Mercurochrome and applied some drops before covering the laceration with a couple of Band-Aids.

After mopping up his bloodied mess, he poked his head out of the doorway and could hear his mother sobbing - he didn't give a damn because if it weren't for Annie, he would have choked the life out of her miserable soul.

Quiet as a field mouse, Loren silently tiptoed to the solitude of his room and secured the door behind him.

Exhausted from the depleted adrenaline rush, he plopped onto the ruffled bed and stared at the ceiling until he fell into a fitful sleep.

IN THE MIDDLE of the night, a sharp

spasm jolted him from his slumber. He sat upright and rotated his arm several times to loosen the throbbing deltoid that absorbed most of the blows.

Fully awake, he got up and began to pace the floor, contemplating what to do next - the clamoring sounds in his head urged him to move out and get away from the psychotic woman he called Mother. For Loren, it was the hardest decision he ever made. He had to go.

In the wee hours, after packing his clothes and a few valuables, he padded to the kitchen and swiped the key ring to his grandmother's car and loaded the trunk of her '54 Ford.

Heart thumping, he backed the clunker out of the carport and rumbled up the graveled alleyway toward Clinton Street.

A combination of excitement and fear coursed through him making his way out of the deteriorating neighborhood - he had never lived alone, always under the strict control of his domineering mother.

THE LUMINOUS DIAL on the dashboard clock displayed five-thirty as Loren pulled into the parking lot of Tiny Naylor's, an all-night eatery on Wilshire and Virgil.

Prior to entering, he purchased a copy

of the Morning Edition of the Los Angeles Examiner from the self-serve rack fastened to the building.

Inside the diner, he noticed three men sitting at the counter, each hunkered over a cup of steaming-hot coffee. Based on their shabby attire, he assumed they were street-people who regularly camped out at the nearby MacArthur Park, a haven for the homeless and hopeless.

The lone graveyard-shift server magically emerged from the prep kitchen, straightening out her service uniform.

Loren captured her attention with a nod while cutting toward a U-shaped booth next to a large picture window.

With amused interest, he gave her the once-over as she sauntered up to him: *mid-forties, most likely divorced and saddled with teenagers to raise, caked-on makeup and a mop of shocking henna-dyed red hair teased high enough to accommodate a nest of wrens.*

She stood over the table with a hand on her hip, clacking her wad of gum nosily while casting furtive glances at his bandage.

"That's quite a lump you got, handsome," she said with a broad smile, displaying a mouthful of equine choppers. "My name's Marilyn. What can I do for you this morning?"

*Horny slut, he thought. Worthless whore.*

With a sneer of disdain, he blocked her view with the menu and requested black coffee, a strip steak cooked bloody rare, eggs sunny side up, hash browns, and wheat toast. After placing his order, he looked up at her and said icily, "I'm done. You can go now."

Put off by the rude customer, Marilyn's face flushed but held her tongue in check, reminding herself: *Suck it up, girl. Every tip counts and Mary Lou needs braces.*

Minutes later, she brought his food and scurried away from the good-looking stranger without saying a word.

Leisurely munching on his breakfast and downing several cups of coffee thick as molasses, Loren perused the classifieds section of the newspaper. He spotted well over a dozen 'For Rent' ads within his budget and circled them with a pen.

By the time he finished his meal and paid the bill without leaving a tip, it was nearly eight.

The better part of the morning was spent driving past various rentals in the Westlake district, most of them in undesirable neighborhoods known for their high rate of vandalism and burglaries.

Unable to locate anything suitable, he broadened his search toward the southwestern fringe of Hollywood.

Out of desperation, he finally settled on a compact apartment the size of a U-Haul truck near Highland and Santa Monica Blvd.

The furnished unit included a kitchenette with a hot plate, a mini-refrigerator that made gurgling noises every few minutes, a worn sleeper-sofa scarcely big enough for three people, and a small B&W Motorola with broken rabbit-ears nestled in a corner of the cheaply decorated room.

After signing a rental agreement and writing a check for the first month's rent, he transferred his belongings to his new home.

Later that same afternoon, he drove to his old house only to find his mother at the kitchen table nibbling on the remnants of a tuna-fish sandwich.

Soon as he walked in, she pummeled him with rapid-fire questions: "Where in the hell have you been! All your things are gone," she cried out. "And who gave you permission to take your grandmother's car?"

Amid the shrieking, he reigned in his

nerves and calmly revealed he had found another place to live but refused to say where.

She stared at him, thunderstruck, chewing feverishly on her bottom lip.

Not giving her the opportunity to go off the deep end, he tenderly pecked her cheek, then turned and bolted out the front door and kept running until he reached the bus stop three blocks away.

Ten minutes later, he hopped a ride that dropped him off walking distance to his new digs.


AFTER SETTLING IN, it didn't take long to find employment as a box-boy at a nearby supermarket, but as the weeks passed, each as boring as the next, he realized new-found freedom had a price - unsettling solitude.

On days off, he often roamed the streets, browsing the eclectic storefronts along the boulevards. At night he'd watch TV or read philosophy and physiology books borrowed from the library.

Over the years, he accepted that he was different from other guys, first aware of it at thirteen - most boys relished sports, girls, fast cars, and rock and roll, while he preferred critical thinking, classical music, and the Arts.

Without friends to confide in, he grew increasingly despondent, and one day gave in to the urge to call his mother - he missed their intimacy.

The sound of her voice instantly soothed him when she answered. With eyes closed, he savored her presence and memories of them snuggling in bed.

"Hello," she repeated to a hollow line. "Who's there?"

*It's me!* he wanted to say, but shook his head to clear the vision and pressed down on the receiver.

The following month Loren called again but this time he didn't hang up.

Once he uttered her name aloud, they conversed for nearly an hour as though nothing had happened between them, and when he got off the phone, he felt relief they were on speaking terms once more.

With their relationship rekindled, she phoned him frequently; the last call ending with her begging him to return, promising she would change her ways.

Not long after, he eventually caved into her and moved back home.

No matter how grotesque their bond, as an adult he understood why she had become his emotional security blanket.

From what he gleaned as a child during their many intimate talks, her deviancy toward him began just before his father abandoned them.

In the months that followed her husband's abrupt departure, Eleanor seduced young Loren into becoming her surrogate lover. She tutored, dominated, and controlled his very being, and as he matured, their mutual attachment flourished exponentially.

However, unbeknownst to her, it was during his thirteenth year that he experienced a life-altering encounter with an eight-year-old neighbor - a turning point when he discovered his predilection for children. Over the years, his feelings intensified, forcing him to create a hedonistic fantasy world he kept secret - a place where rational thought ceased to exist, supplanted by a chimera of unnatural desires....

**★★★★**

LOREN BLINKED SEVERAL times, snapping him back to the present - seated at the kitchen table, still fuming from his mother's backhand.

*You should've killed her years ago,* said one of the surly inner voices deep in his psyche.

Jaw clenched, his volatile temper continued to percolate until another personality bubbled to the surface, it's mellow tone forever comforting: *You know she can't help herself. She's unstable, so hold off until you move to the hideaway. Then you can kill her.*

Loren nodded in agreement.

"Moth-er!" he protested, recalculating his course of action. "I'm not looking at pictures of women," pointing to the pile of prints. "It's from work. See?"

Quick as a rattlesnake strike, her hand lashed out and hit him flush on the face.

THWACK!

"Don't you ever talk back to me, Miss ... Miss ... Lana Turner!" she shrieked before turning and storming out of the room, shouting over her shoulder: "You just remember what I told you. Stay away from other women!"

"You forgot to take your fucking meds today, didn't you!" he hollered.

The snarky comment went unanswered.

With a woeful sigh and a shake of his head, he returned to the task at hand, focusing his concern to the illustrations on the table.

Two of the inserts were blown-up replicas of a street map projecting one-way routes of major thoroughfares and freeways underscored with red lines. At some intersections, green arrows indicated the direction heading along a north-easterly path toward the City of Pasadena. A black star pinpointed the end at a location on Fair Oaks Avenue.

Minutes later he heard footsteps approaching and hurriedly rolled up the diagrams just before his mother walked in.

"Put that garbage away because dinners about ready," she snapped, her arms waving in the air like a crazed orchestra conductor. "You're always messing up my kitchen with your crap. I'm not your maid, you big dummy!"

Loren eased up from the chair and stood in front of her, and at six foot four, glowered down with contempt.

Startled by his menacing look, she spun away and disappeared into the pantry, cursing under her breath.

With the materials tucked under his arm, he trudged to his private sanctuary and unlocked the door.

The pungent scent of printer's ink greeted him crossing the threshold, and he inhaled the aroma with a welcoming familiarity before securing the door behind him.

Inside, scores of charts and renderings were pinned to every wall. Some depicted floor plans of a single-family dwelling with detached garage, while others bore sketches of the front and back seats of his '57 Chevy from numerous angles.

Nearest the only window, the drawings pictured even more details; blow-ups of a woman's vanity case rigged with clamps and a three-speed bicycle handbrake.

Stacks of reading material sat in piles on the carpet. Many were texts on psychology, others with assorted titles for specific purposes, like: "Weapons and Their Uses," "Handguns," and "Dissection of the Human Anatomy."

Atop the nightstand, sat a frayed typewritten seventy-one page manifesto entitled, "God, Man, and the Devil," by L.R.Neestrom.

Setting his manuscript aside, he reached under the saggy bed and pulled out a rectangular cardboard box.

Rummaging through the contents, he picked out a pair of chrome-plated handcuffs with the tag and two keys still hanging from the end of a stringed knot.

"Loren! Get in here, now!" Eleanor barked. "Supper is ready."

Annoyed by the interruption: "Yes, Moth-er. Right away Moth-er," he replied, and slid the container back to its hiding place.

On the way to the kitchen he thought, *Where's the lease for the house in Pasadena?* Then he remembered; the paperwork was in the Chevy's glove compartment, safe and out of the way.

He strolled into the room and eyed his mother at the stove, clad with a soiled red and white checkered apron tied around her narrow waist.

She heard him enter and turned to give him a nasty once-over.

"Wake up! You're always walking around like you're in a daydream," she nagged. "How many times have I told you to quit slouching? Stand straight like a concert pianist, head erect..." then she went silent for a beat and her frown morphed into a sly grin, "...and we know how erect you can be, you naughty, naughty boy."

Loren froze mid-step and his nostrils flared. Defiant, he flipped her the bird, did an abrupt about-face, and headed to the foyer in a huff.

"Where the hell do you think you're going! What about the food on the table?" she yelled, her captivating blue eyes flashing wildly. "Come back here, you bastard! I didn't cook this shit for nothing."

Suddenly her demeanor changed: "Oh baby, don't be mad at me," she cooed. "You know how I get sometimes. What if I give you a bath tonight after Annie leaves? One of our special ones," she said, batting her eyelashes. "The kind you always like. Hmm?"

He growled at her with disdain, seething with resentment — her cherished *boy-toy* belonged to him, and if she wanted his appendage, she'd have to wait until he was good and ready.

Without a word, he snatched his blue denim jacket from the antique coatrack and slipped it on.

"Hey mister, what the hell do you think you're doing?" she screeched, running her hands through her hair.

Paying little attention to her antics, he stormed out and slammed the door.

The moment he stepped on the front stoop, a wry smile tugged at the corners of

his mouth - he relished the notion of her
stuck in the house throwing a hissy-fit.

   *Fuck her! She'll get hers when the time*
*comes.*

# CHAPTER 2

**THE HIDEAWAY**
July, 1961

WITH A REVITALIZED spring to his gait,
he trotted the short block-and-a-half to his
car.

In the twilight, the black '57 Chevy
Bel Air blended into the street, its color
indistinguishable at night. The odometer
displayed 40,350 miles when he purchased it
from a smooth-talking dealer in North
Hollywood three months earlier. Aside from a
broken horn, there were no dents or dings,
and the silver tuck-and-roll upholstery
appeared to be in pristine condition.

Loren opened the passenger door first
and slid across the seat in one fluid
movement.

Relaxed, he gazed at the two-by-four
mounted on the dash, and patted it with his
fingertips.

"Soitently is brilliant! Sometimes I
even amaze meself ... yuk, yuk, yuk," he
trilled in Curly Joe falsetto, imitating his
favorite of the Three Stooges.

Then he began to laugh aloud, his guffaws growing in intensity. Even the voices in his head joined in, howling in unison.

After a few minutes of out-of-control cackling, he wiped the tears from his eyes as he regained his senses and turned his attention to the side door and window handles - a week before, he loosened the hex screw of each, rendering them inoperable.

"Once inside ... ain't no way out," he chirped, and cracked his knuckles one by one, visualizing the image of a giant spider gazing at a fly trapped helplessly in its intricate web.

With a nod of approval, he backed out and walked to the driver's side, furtively glancing over his shoulder to make sure nobody was spying on him.

Satisfied no one was watching, he scooted behind the wheel and fired up the throaty V-8, then goosed the gas pedal a couple of times before peeling away from the curb.

LOST IN THOUGHT while navigating Highway 101 toward Pasadena, Loren reminisced how he had spent months checking out affordable homes to lease before settling on the 1920s single-story clapboard house.

Luck was on his side when he noticed an ad in the classified section of the Star-News, captioned: "Secluded and perfect for young couples. Monthly rent, $300.00."

The partially furnished home consisted of two large bedrooms, a spacious living room with adjoining dining area, and one bath.

He recalled how his pulse had quickened when the owner showed him around the outside of the property.

"I'll take it!" Loren said eagerly," replaying the scene of his conversation with the elderly gentleman. "But I'll only need it for six months because I'm planning on enlisting in the Navy," he lied.

"That'll be fine," the landlord replied. "I'm an old Army-guy, myself. Fought in WWI. One helluva war, son. Consider yourself lucky we're in peacetime," he said with a tortured smile, his eyes registering horrific memories.

"Oh, by the way, the utilities are included. And I'll leave you the push mower, too," he added, pointing a gnarly finger at the grassy expanse.

The withered old-timer hesitated, and his hooded eyes welled. "Since the missus passed, I haven't had much energy these days." Then he gestured with his head toward the house: "She died on our bed while I was out buying her some ice cream. Dang-it-all, we sure shared great times here," he said after wiping his nose with the back of his forearm. "Just take care of the place. That's all I ask."

Several days after signing the rental agreement, Loren re-inspected his hideaway at 2014 Fair Oaks without anyone at his side.

Two of the five rooms were adequately decorated with inexpensive accent pieces and the oak flooring had been cleaned and recently polished.

He strolled room-to-room and detected the tell-tale smell of cigarettes mingled with the faint scent of mothballs and Ben-Gay, three odors reminiscent of his grandmother that made him feel at home.

On his way to the back of the house, he paused at the bathroom and stared at the freestanding clawfoot tub. Pleasant thoughts dribbled through his memory, imagining himself becoming the teacher again as it was with his eight-year-old neighbor, Johnny.

Anxious for a peek of his surroundings, he opened the screen door and surveyed the backyard from the elevated stoop.

Off to his left, a narrow driveway led to a dilapidated oversized wood-frame garage the size of a mini warehouse. To his right, a plot of freshly mowed St. Augustine with lush beds of purple and white geraniums lining either side were surrounded by tall rows of flowering pink oleanders separating the lot from adjacent properties.

From his vantage point, the fenced yard offered plenty of distance between adjoining neighbors, providing the seclusion he needed.

He stepped down to the pathway leading to the weather-beaten garage, and when he depressed the thumb-latch on the door and tugged on the handle, the corroded side-mounted brackets squealed in protest and the metal wheels grated loudly rolling over the coarse pavement.

Like fingernails being dragged across a blackboard, the hair on his arms stood-on-end. Irked, he fished a pen and scrap of paper from his chambray shirt pocket and scribbled the words: LUBRICATE HINGES AND ROLLERS!

**✱✱✱✱**

*IF MOTHER ONLY knew I had a secret home, she'd go ballistic*, Loren mused while passing through the Arroyo Seco tunnels on his way to Pasadena.

With spirits soaring, he hummed Gershwin's Rhapsody in Blue, tapping the chrome horn rim as though his fingers were softly stroking piano keys. The exercise brought back fond recollections of practicing daily after school until his hands ached - he had become so skillful, his instructors gushed that he had the potential to be a concert pianist; a *child prodigy,* they said.

He wondered if he might ever achieve the lofty goal, even at twenty-four. *Maybe I still can?* he thought and reminded himself to find a music store to rent a used spinet. *It'll fit perfectly next to one of the bay windows.*

As he approached his clandestine residence on Fair Oaks, Loren turned left into the driveway and eased the Chevy up the sloped apron and came to a stop behind the house. His eyes followed the headlight beams casting yellowish circles over the hedges on the far side of the lot.

With the transmission in neutral, he got out and unlatched the garage door. It opened with ease. *Oiling the joints and duct-taping the rollers eliminated most of the grating noise,* he nodded, pleased with his resourcefulness.

Returning to the car, he nosed into the moldy wooden edifice and killed the engine, then sat motionless listening to the rhythmic chirping of crickets coming back to life.

Moments later he got out and shut the door and switched off the headlamps.

"Pitch-black like a tomb," he uttered scanning the cavernous void, his eyes adapting to the darkness with uncanny speed.

The details of the musty interior gradually came into view: the exposed slats over tar paper walls, bags of concrete, and the lawnmower off in one corner.

Switching the headlights back on, he popped the trunk and removed two sixty-pound sacks of Redi-Mix cement and piled them on top of others from previous trips.

After closing the lid, a gravelly voice in his head whispered, *Now the hunt begins....*

# CHAPTER 3

**THE BOYS**
Summer, 1961

SPENDING DAYS AT Muscle Beach throughout the summer had become a ritual for the five close friends.

At least three times a week, Steve and Rick would meet up with Glen, Jeff and Jack on the corner of Olympic and Robertson at nine in the morning and thumb a ride to the Pacific Ocean. It usually took them less than half-an-hour to get to the historic blue and white gateway-arch over the Santa Monica Pier, famously known as the end of Route 66.

Although the skies were often overcast when they arrived, the guys would find their patch of nirvana well above the water's edge to scope out chicks strolling the shore once the heat burned away the fog.

After the boys claimed their slice of prime real estate, they'd spread out on towels and spend the day basking under the sun while playing every conceivable form of poker - the antes typically ranged from nickels and dimes, with some pots growing as high as twenty-five dollars.

Other than gambling and ogling girls, body surfing was their beach-going pastime.

Every so often, someone would yell: "Outside!" Card-playing would cease momentarily as heads popped up, scanning the Pacific for massive rollers forming at what appeared to be the earth's horizon. If the advancing set grew in height, they would dash into the water with hopes of catching the perfect wave.

**★★★★**

HE SHOULD HAVE been concentrating on his poker hand but rubbernecking the shoreline packed with girls, Steve allowed his thoughts to drift.

Nearby, a transistor radio tuned to KFWB blared the No. 1 hit song, *Runaround Sue*. The image of his girlfriend flashed before him and vanished just as quickly when he spotted an exquisite gem heading in his direction.

The beauty couldn't have been more than seventeen, but the way she moved led him to believe she could be a lot younger.

In the skimpiest of bikinis - mere strips of fabric - her breasts rose and fell as though they were swells on a gentle sea while her silky blonde hair flowed in the breeze like a Palomino's mane at full gallop.

Lying prone on the warm sand, fighting the sudden stirring in his groin, he was thankful his back faced the sun lest he demonstrate to his buddies his lack of loin'al control.

As she sauntered by, she offered up a thin smile.

*Damn, she is gorgeous*, he thought, staring at her perfectly curved backside as she strutted toward the surf.

She stopped briefly and playfully peeked over her shoulder to see if he was still gawking.

*Holy shit! Did she just wink?* he half-wondered, half-hoped. For a fleeting moment, he considered it an invitation to chase after her.

*Maybe I should....*

"Earth calling Horndog! Wipe the drool from your mouth, dipshit. You've already got a main squeeze, and in case you forgot, you called my bet," Jeff Finestein croaked, his distinctive raspy voice snapping Steve back to the hand of Seven-card Stud.

Only three players remained in the high-stakes game. Glen and Jack folded earlier and decided to go show off on the gymnastic equipment near the bustling strand.

"I've got a full boat, aces over eights," Rick blurted out-of-turn, overly excited he might be holding the winning hand.

"Sonofabitch! That beats the hell out of me," Jeff snorted, his gravelly voice sounding as though he'd been smoking for fifty years. "Now I'm really depressed," he said, springing to his feet. "I think I'm going to join the other losers," then he turned and trudged toward the trapeze-like apparatus embedded in concrete footings, cursing to himself while dragging his towel behind him like a prehensile tail.

Steve watched his dejected pal kick up a shower of sand, making his way to the towering crossbar of the swinging rings adjacent to what had once been the Muscle Beach arena.

He reflected to his childhood days when the workout pit was filled with brawny men lifting free-weights resembling manhole covers; their rippling flesh and sweaty bodies had long since disappeared after the city closed the facilities in 1959.

A sly grin stretched across Rick's face as he turned to his cohort and demanded to see his hand.

Even though Steve had been dealt a full house, it wasn't strong enough to win. He gazed at the mound of coins and bills and estimated the kitty held well over twenty bucks.

"Fuck-a-duck. All I have is tens over kings," he hissed, and threw his last hold card face-up on the blanket. "I sure hope the rest of the week isn't this shitty."

Rick's smile broadened.

"There goes the money I needed to take Sue to see The Guns of Navarone Thursday night. I'll be sure to tell her it was all your fault, A-hole."

"Screw you!" Rick chortled while greedily scooping up the cash. "Putting me on a guilt trip ain't gonna work this time, amigo." Then he paused a beat as though an idea suddenly flittered into his head.

"Tell you what. Think of a hot junior from Fairfax High that you can hook me up with, and if we go out on a double date, it'll be my treat. How 'bout them apples?"

"Seriously?"

Rick nodded.

"Okay, you're on, putz," the timing ideal for ensnaring his gullible friend.

Shaking out a cigarette from his pack of Marlboro's, he took his time packing it down on his thumbnail, and then put his trusty Zippo to work.

After a few puffs, he locked eyes with his sidekick. "What if I can get you together with, um, let me think for a second," he said teasingly, mulling over a list of names that would elicit an outrageous outburst.

"Wait!" he finally said. "How about Claudia Silverman?"

"Whaaat! Are you out of your freaking mind?" Rick barked. "I wouldn't be caught dead with an oinker like her. She's ugly as all get-out, her face resembles the surface of the moon, and her choppers look like they belong on a cud-chewing beast. Besides, someone told me she's frigid."

"Okay! Okay! Give it a rest, Steve said, holding back the overwhelming urge to laugh while goading his pal into an ambush.

He took another deep drag and French-inhaled, watching the smoke waft from his mouth to his nostrils.

"All right, that's one strike against me. Let's try another babe who might meet your ... uh ... exceptionally high standards."

Moments later he cried out: "I've got it! Marsha Cohen. She's got a beautiful complexion, a terrific personality, and she's loose as a goose."

"Blow it out your ass!" Rick bellowed loud enough to be heard by everyone within earshot. "Do you think I'm a fucking farmer? Marsha's wazoo is the size of a barn! If you stood behind her while she jogged, the cheeks of her butt are so big, you'd think you were watching two VW's drag-racing, trying to pass each other. C'mon man, quit screwing around!"

Nearby, a gaggle of eavesdropping teenyboppers broke out in giggles. One of them, all freckles and teeth, clapped her hands applauding the hysterical retort.

"Hey! There's people who can hear you so cut the gas and check your language! Steve blurted. "I'm done messing around. Scout's honor," holding up the three-fingered salute.

To extend the theatrics, he rested his chin on the heel of his palm pretending to be lost in thought, ready to spring the trap.

After a melodramatic pause: "What about ... Melanie?" he whispered, his voice barely audible - he knew his best friend had a crush on her but was too shy to do anything about it. What his buddy didn't know was that he too, had the hots for her.

Rick's jaw dropped - the mere mention of her name knotted his gut.

"Whoa. I wasn't ready for *that*," he uttered as though the wind had been knocked out of him.

"Tell you what," he squinted skeptically, "Fix me up with her and I'll treat you to any of Wan-Q's Special Cantonese dinners and the movies. Take your pick: The Stadium, the Lido, or the Picfair Theater." Then he stole a quick peek at his pile of winnings, and added, "And because I'm feeling generous now, I'll even toss in buttered popcorn. How's that for incentive?"

*Got him!* Steve thought. *Dinner and a Flick. Far better than I expected.*

"Tis good as done me lad," he replied in his best brogue imitation, knowing Sue had recently persuaded Melanie to meet Rick on a blind date.

"Next Saturday night, my naïve little friend, you and I will be at Sue's house."

"Huh?"

"Does September 16th ring a bell? Remember when I told you her parents will be at an all-night party?"

"Yeah. So what am I supposed to be doing while you two are busy in her bedroom swapping spit?"

"Guess who else will be there?" Steve said with a mischievous smirk. "Melanie."

# CHAPTER 4

**THE FINAL DETAIL**
August 31, 1961

"SORRY," SAID BILL Seeley, the elderly proprietor of Westward Blueprinting. "I've got to lay you off."

Blindsided, Loren's face went slack.

"Kid, you're a good worker but business has slowed down dramatically over the past several months, and since you got the least amount of seniority, well..."

"But..."

"I'm truly sorry," the old man reiterated, his weathered face registering a spark of compassion. He removed his thick metal-frame bifocals, revealing a notched indentation on the bridge of his nose, and said, "Believe me, there was no choice."

A bead of sweat broke out between Loren's shoulder blades, and his hands trembled. *Laid off? I was just going to ask for a raise to help cover the expense for my secret hideaway.*

Rattled, he tried to corral the rush
of panic surging through him and shoved his
clenched fists into his pockets.

"Hey, you're a multi-talented guy,"
Bill cajoled in an effort to smooth things
over. "With your penchant for detail, I'm
sure you'll find employment in no time. Now
go see the bookkeeper," he motioned, hooking
a thumb toward the back of the building,
"and she'll give you your severance. I told
her to toss in two weeks additional pay to
tide you over until you find some work."

With a feeble smile of gratitude, Loren
nodded and walked away, his brain
calculating the loss of steady income.

After stripping off his coveralls and
hanging them on the rack with the other ink-
stained aprons, he zigzagged his way through
the maze of printing presses toward the
cluttered business office.

Fresh out of UCLA, Sonia tended to her
accounting chores with mature efficiency.
According to the scuttlebutt, many co-
workers deemed the hot-looking twenty-two-
year-old untouchable, off-limits due to her
familial relationship with the owner.

At five-foot eight, she was striking to
behold. With wide-set hazel eyes and long
raven hair cascading over her shoulders like
a sable shawl, her sculpted beauty made men
turn their heads.

"I'll miss seeing everyone here,"
Loren uttered sheepishly, standing in front
of her desk, shifting from one foot to the
other - most females made him extremely
nervous.

"Oh no you won't," she retorted with a
twinge of sadness.

Little did he know how much she would
miss seeing his beautiful face every day -
exceptionally tall, his chiseled features
and wholesome appearance captivated her from
the moment she first laid eyes on him.
Unlike the crass men she worked with in the
plant, he didn't display the typical vices
like smoking or cursing in her presence and
he seemed to possess an inner feminine
quality she found appealing and refreshing.

Over the past year, she tried in vain
to seduce him, but he never responded to her
outrageous innuendos. At one point she
thought he might have been queer but
sloughed off the notion - he was simply too
good-looking not to be interested in women.
Especially her.

She stood up from behind the desk and
leaned over while handing him an envelope
with his earnings - the upper three buttons
of her plaid blouse were intentionally
unfastened, exposing her Frederick's of
Hollywood lace pushup bra.

The moment Loren gazed at the ample

curve of her breasts, his mother's words quickly echoed in his head: *"Stay away from women. They'll destroy you like they did your father."*

"Ahem," Sonia cleared her throat with an impish flicker in her eyes, pleased with generating a reaction.

"You'll call me, won't you?" she urged, easing back on the rickety secretarial chair. "And since you're not an employee anymore, thanks to my uncle, maybe we could get together for some fun. My treat."

"Sounds terrific. Give me a week or two," Loren lied, knowing it would never happen. *She'd freak out if she knew the real me.*

More important issues filled his head after leaving the room and weaving through the rows of thumping machinery.

Even with the burden of his rental, he felt confident of finding a job near Pasadena where he could zip home for lunch to keep an eye on things - a corner of his mouth rose as the recurring fantasy of a naked child strapped spread-eagle to bedposts popped into his thoughts.

In a less frazzled state, he ambled to the front counter.

"See ya, Mr. Seeley. I hope business

picks up for you real soon. And by the way, I sure appreciate the extra money. Thanks again."

"Best of luck to you, son," the man replied, shaking Loren's hand with a firm grip. "Give us a call if there's anything else we can do."

THE GLOWING WARMTH of the afternoon sun enveloped him as he stepped outside. Loren sucked in a deep breath welcoming the sweet briny scent from the nearby Pacific Ocean, a stark contrast to the acrid odors inside the print shop.

The stoplight at Barrington Avenue turned green, and while crossing the busy intersection, he peered at the mirror-tinted windows of the Thomas Building as he strolled by. The image staring back revealed a handsome, well-built young man clad in tan chinos and long-sleeve denim work shirt.

He flashed a killer smile at his reflection, mindful most women were attracted to him, often ogling with lust-filled eyes. But that wasn't what he wanted.

*The Becoming of One*, a feral voice in his head murmured.

With no intention of returning home an hour early, he drove to the military surplus store with hopes of finding a few items for his list.

Fifteen minutes later, he spotted the familiar free-standing brick warehouse on Venice near Culver City and pulled into the parking lot.

In short order, he found two woolen military blankets and a couple of canvas duffel bags with U.S. ARMY stenciled on each side.

After paying the cashier, he strode out of the cavernous building and tossed his goods onto the back seat, then decided to take the long way home.


"WELL, IF IT isn't Miss Lana Turner," Eleanor quipped while giving Loren a nasty once-over. With a sarcastic "humph," she turned back to the pot of beef stew simmering on the stove.

*Uh-oh. She's in rare form tonight,* Loren thought, and opted not to tell her about losing his job - she'd take it as a sign of weakness.

"Stop calling me that woman's name! You know how much I hate it," he fired back. "Would you've preferred a daughter, or do you despise me because I'm the spitting likeness of dad?"

Eleanor's harsh cackle resonated

through the room - it was a mean laugh brimming with contempt. She wiped her hands on her apron and reached for the half-empty glass of Johnny Walker.

"Of course I wanted a baby girl, dummy. More than anything in the world. But when the doctor told me I couldn't have any children after *you*," she said, emphasizing the word with deep-seated resentment, "I blamed your father. The male seed he squirted in me screwed up my life."

Stunned, Loren said, "Is that why you liked dressing me as a girl when I was little?"

His mother almost spilled her drink.

"Here's what you don't know Mister Smarty Pants. You were only two or three and won't recall the incident," she scowled, reliving the moment in time.

"One day your father came home from work earlier than expected and you were dolled up in the cutest dress with lipstick and eye makeup on. Well, the prick wigged out and beat the living shit out of me. Put me in the hospital for a few days."

Her eyes welled. "All I ever wanted in life was a daughter ... and instead, I got *you*!"

Suddenly her demeanor changed, and she

smiled that wicked smile he'd seen so many times.

"Sweetie, I'm sorry I said those horrible things. Gaw'd Almighty, haven't you realized by now there are moments when I'm glad you're a strong, gorgeous young man. The way you feel..." then her voice plunged to a sultry whisper, "...the way you make me come alive."

She took another gulp of her drink and smacked her lips. "Not like your dad. Besides, you're far more attractive and *bigger*, if you get what I mean," glancing at his crotch. "Just remember: No messing around with other women like your father," she snapped as her mood did an abrupt one-eighty. "They're all whores, you hear. The whole lot of 'em!"

"What's with all the shouting?"

Loren spun around as Annie waddled into the kitchen clad in a terry bathrobe with a hairnet over her pink curlers.

"Grandma," he whined, greeting her with a look of pained frustration. "She's doing her psycho routine on me," then he distorted his face, mimicking his mother, and his voice ratcheted to a shriek with arms flailing like a madman.

"Women are a bunch of evil filthy sluts, the whole lot of them."

Annie burst out in laughter and clapped her hands, applauding him for his masterful performance. "Not only are you an incredible piano player but a pretty good actor as well."

"You'd be a fine one to talk, MOTH-ER," Eleanor hissed over her shoulder while pouring another two fingers of Scotch. "You'd know all about married men chasing after women ... and precocious little girls!"

Annie's withered cheeks flushed, and she glanced at her grandson: *It's a miracle he turned out so well. So polite and artistic.* Disgusted, she shook her head and prayed for the day when he became a concert pianist and escaped her daughter's malevolent grasp - he had such God-given creative talent and hated seeing it go to waste.

"Try to be patient," she whispered after Eleanor scurried off to the pantry on a quest for a can of stewed tomatoes.

"It won't be long before you find someone special and leave this ... madness ... and have a life of your own. For me, it's too late because someone needs to look after your crazy mother."

Then she gestured with opened arms: "Now get over here you big hunk and give me a hug," she said with a twinkle in her rheumy eyes.

AT SEVEN THE following morning, Loren dressed and ate his usual breakfast of a bowl of Cheerio's with half a sliced banana, then left the house as though going to work.

Rather than heading west, he jumped on the eastbound lane of the congested Hollywood Freeway and veered onto the Glendale cutoff. From there, he crossed Foothill Boulevard and cruised through the exclusive communities of La Canada-Flintridge and the start of the Angeles Crest Highway.

The tree-lined road with custom-built homes staged against the backdrop of pristine mountaintops soon gave way to timbered foothills where the morning air was crisp and the sky an azure blue. A vivid contrast to the crowded asphalt jungle below.

On the way up the hill, he thought about his mission for the day. Only two items remained unfinished on the Project List: the first and most important, pinpoint a suitable area remote and craggy - he recalled spotting a potential location on one of his previous trips up the mountainside and hoped to find it again.

The Chevy climbed the steep turnpike, downshifting in and out of passing gear, until he eyed a dirt trail leading off-road to a secluded part of the forest.

His heart raced. *Is this the place?*

Turning onto the narrow washboard path, he drove in half a mile and parked where lush spruce and pine trees surrounded him like a tunnel.

With the engine shut down, he got out and walked the grounds, taking note of the granite outcroppings.

*Perfect*, he thought, satisfied his memory served him well.

Back in the car, he opened his notebook and placed a checkmark next to the words: *Disposal Site.*

Nestled amid the peaceful tranquility of nature, he stretched out and listened to one of his favorite radio stations playing a concerto by Ludwig von Beethoven - Loren loved classical music, particularly Chopin, whose haunting *Funeral March Sonata* matched his darker moods.

Twenty minutes later, he got out again and did a slow three-sixty. Convinced there were no hikers nearby, he unlocked the trunk and fetched a brown vinyl-covered cosmetic case made popular by women in the 1950s.

The double-latched rectangular box had

a half-inch round outlet the size of a dime purposely bored through one of the end-panels. From inside, the barrel of a nine-round .22-caliber Harrington & Richardson revolver fit snugly against the small hole.

On the opposite side of the case, Loren had drilled a smaller opening to allow a length of cable to pass through and connect to the caliper of a bicycle brake with the asbestos pads stationed over the trigger. Metal strapping secured the weapon in place and scores of washrags were crammed in the box to stifle the notable bark of gunfire.

With the vanity case set directly behind the passenger seat, he snaked the other end of the cabling underneath the carpeting all the way to the driver's door and connected it to a handbrake attached to an "L" shaped piece of three-quarter-inch lead pipe fastened to the floorboard.

The view out the front window soon became a blur while he gazed blankly at the forested canyon beyond, visualizing in his head the scenario he intended to put into play.

With palms atop his lap, he surreptitiously lowered his left hand, grasped the jerry-rigged lever, and squeezed.

CLICK.

He heard the unmistakable sound of the revolver's hammer striking the empty chamber and repeated the exercise several times.

Content everything functioned as planned, he retrieved a carton of ammo and three, one inch thick twelve-by-twelve plywood slabs from the back of the car.

After some quick mental calculations, he slid two of the wooden squares under the box, then loaded a single round in the cylinder, and closed the lid.

Behind the wheel, he took in a breath and dropped his arm until he touched the makeshift handle. Slowly, he tightened his grip on the rigging.

BANG!

The bullet exploded from the pistol and ripped through the front seat - a neat circle appearing ten inches down from the top.

*Damn! The rags inside really helped muffle the noise*, he thought, even though his ears rang, and his nostrils flared at the distinct smell of expended gunpowder.

On closer inspection, he noticed the copper-jacketed slug buried in the center of the two-by-four mounted on the dash.

"I was right," he hooted. "The

windshield would've cracked without the block. Sometimes I'm so fucking smart it scares me."

Using a flathead screwdriver, he pried the fragment loose, dismantled the gun-device, and returned all the hardware to the trunk.

From the glove compartment, he extracted a roll of black tape and tore off two strips to hide the small punctures in the upholstery and placed several larger pieces marking the exact position of the boards on the backseat.

With all the equipment safely stowed under an army surplus blanket, he wove his way through the hairpin turns downhill to make his last stop of the day — Johnson's Butcher Supply.

It took him less than ten minutes to select the final item on his list; a sixteen-inch meat saw.

# CHAPTER 5

**THE NIGHT BEFORE**
September 15, 1961

STEVE THREW ON a clean pullover, eying his brother on the bed immersed in an Isaac Asimov paperback.

The room they shared had extra-long twin beds and a hefty double-tiered oak bookcase topped with a fifty-gallon aquarium stocked with varieties of large freshwater fish.

An eclectic array of sports memorabilia, Playboy pin-up's, and abstract paintings created by their Aunt Shirley adorned the walls.

"C'mon, bro, tell me. Please! It's important," Steve whined while running a small pocket comb through his lustrous mat of hair. "I gotta know before I go out."

Annoyed by the constant interruptions, twenty-one-year-old Shel put the book aside and stood up, glowering at his young charge.

"Listen to me," he grumbled. "All I'm saying is you're not old enough to be thinking about that shit. For crissakes, you just turned fifteen!"

"Yeah? What about you when you were my age? Like you were some kind of saint?"

"Well, uh, that's different," said Shel, dismissing the retort and quickly changing the subject. "If you're going to use the john, hurry up because I'll need it after you."

The look of disappointment etched on his brother's face hit a soft spot as he reflected on his own exploits as an out-of-control juvenile delinquent.

"Oh, what the hell," Shel finally uttered. "You're just growing up so fucking fast."

Steve's eyes widened.

"Look, I'm simply trying to stop you from making the same mistakes I've made," Shel said. "And your mother and I don't want to worry about you knocking up some chick who's hot-to-trot and having to quit school to support a family. Okay?"

Steve bobbed his head several times.

"Now to answer your question, all you got to do ...."

While his street-savvy mentor pontificated, Steve's inquisitive young mind sponged up every detail. At times like this he appreciated having an older sibling to confide in and learn from, especially when the subject pertained to sex.

"Far out!" he whooped, as eloquent depictions were driven home. "Well, what does it feel like when you ... you know ... pop her cherry?"

Shel chuckled.

"All I can say is once you do the deed, your little head will be in control forever. But make sure you use rubbers," he said as an afterthought. "And not the cheap ones like Sheiks; most of the time they rip apart. Remember what happened to Harry's ex-girlfriend, Georgia?"

Steve recalled the tense days following her botched abortion in Tijuana; the ensuing complications from the Mexican butcher pretending to be a doctor nearly killed her.

"Tell you what," said Shel. "There's a dozen 4X's in my dresser drawer. I'll let you borrow some, but you got to pay me back because they're expensive as hell. Like two bucks apiece" - even though they cost a dollar for a three-pack he figured he should make a profit giving that kind of advice. "Repay me from next week's allowance."

Armed with newfound knowledge, Steve dashed to the bathroom to re-comb his hair for the umpteenth time.

"Crap! Got to split," Shel yelled down the long hallway after glancing at his watch. "I'm supposed to pick up Howard from work and give him a lift. The *Blue Monster* broke down again."

Not hearing a response, he barged into the room, only to find his brother still primping, getting his jellyroll and ducktail shaped right.

"Your hair's perfect Lover-Boy, so move your ass," he barked. "By the way, if you're going to work out tonight, be home by ten. Not ten-thirty. Not ten-fifteen. Ten o'clock, or else. Got it?"

Oblivious to the ominous warning, Steve crossed his heart, and then leaned in to catch one more glimpse in the mirror of his Jay Sebring pompadour.

Satisfied, he made a hasty beeline out of the apartment and jogged the few short blocks to his favorite hangout.

**★★★★**

A HAVEN FOR local youth, the Robertson Recreation Center sat on a triangular-shaped lot strategically divided into three distinct sections: on the narrowest tip, small children had their play area with a merry-go-round, swing sets, teeter-totters, and a metal mini-slide.

Most of the teenagers hung out at the widest side of the park with basketball and volleyball courts outlined in white paint over coarse asphalt.

For wannabe gymnasts, a thirty by fifty-foot rectangular sandpit with concrete edging had been built along the portion fronting Preuss Rd. It contained steel parallel bars, a jungle gym, and towering swinging rings anchored by massive pylons.

And for hoop aficionado's, there was a vaulted indoor gymnasium with a hardwood court and several adjoining hobby rooms built in the center of the irregular-shaped parcel of land.

Six-foot-high chain link fencing enclosed the entire perimeter, and floodlights set on autotimers illuminated the grounds at dusk. Mature elm trees offered an abundance of shade during the heat of day, and at night, the thick branches served as wonderful hiding places for kids playing hide-and-seek.

**★★★★**

HE SPOTTED SOME of his card-playing chums sitting by the pit, gawking at Jackie, a cute twelve-year-old tomboy who lived in the house next to Steve's apartment building.

Hanging upside down on a parallel bar by the crook of her knees, she swayed back and forth with her eyes closed, seemingly without a care in the world.

With long silken-blonde hair draped like a curtain, she was unaware her tee-shirt had pulled away from her waistband, revealing a tanned mid-section and the entirety of her flimsy white training bra.

What captured the attention of the sex-crazed boys were her budding breasts pressed against the ultra-sheer fabric.

Glen yanked the Marlboro from his mouth when he saw his buddy approaching and put a finger to his lips, motioning with his head toward the girl.

Steve glanced in her direction and quickly got the gist of what was taking place.

"Whatcha all looking at?" he said loudly, trying to alert his brazen neighbor.

Jackie's eyes popped open at the sound of his voice — she had a major crush on him but knew he only thought of her as a coming-of-age teenybopper. One day she hoped to change his mind.

"Aw, fuck-a-duck!" Jack roared. "You just spoiled our fun."

"Say cutie! Why don't you unhook your little-girl harness and give us a real show?" Jeff croaked in his distinctive voice. "You're only about a cup size from being grown up."

The instant she heard his words, Jackie realized her top had slipped down, exposing her bra. Embarrassed, she leaped from her perch and charged the four clowns like a bull elephant, shouting expletives that would make a sailor blush.

The boys howled uncontrollably; Jeff with tears running down his freckled cheeks, his hands clutching his aching belly.

The laughter was infectious, and Steve struggled not to join in on the zany raunchiness.

After a few moments of macho revelry, Rick stopped snickering and apologized. Shortly thereafter, the remaining stooges half-heartedly begged forgiveness, all on their haunches prostrating profusely while giggling among themselves.

Humiliated, Jackie tucked in her shirt and sidled up to Rick to share his cigarette.

Reluctantly, he handed it to her, and as she puffed away, he couldn't take his eyes off her boobs, the outline of the perky headlamps still fresh in his mind.

Filled with a lingering giddiness, Jeff wiped the dampness from his face with the back of his forearm and announced that Rick did a double somersault for the very first time earlier in the evening.

Like a proud tutor, Steve shuffled over to praise his best friend.

"Hey putz. Take your eyes off her tits for a second."

Just as he was about to offer up another snide comment, Glen sidled up to him and tapped him on the shoulder.

"All right Mr. Hot Stuff. Didn't you say if Rick got the nerve to do a double, you'd do a triple? So..." he posed arrogantly, "...are you going to chicken out?"

"You're a real prick," Steve said, shooting him a scathing look of contempt - he hated being goaded into doing things he didn't want to do, even though he recollected making the challenge to motivate his clumsy pal.

*Boy, I really got suckered into that*, he thought.

After mustering his courage, he removed his sneakers and socks without a word and stepped inside the familiar arena.

The grains scrunching under his bare feet helped soothe his jittery nerves ... until he tilted his head back and viewed the crossbar looming high above. Dread crept into in his gut. No one in his circle of acrobat-savvy friends ever attempted three somersaults without using a spotter's belt.

*You can do this*, he re-affirmed, working up his confidence while chalking his calloused hands with a bar of calcium carbonate. *You've done doubles hundreds of times. Besides, you can't back out now. Not with everybody watching.*

With a nod to no one in particular, he jumped up and caught the thick suspended rings and asked Jack, the strongest of the group, to give him a hard push.

Like a trapeze artist, Steve attained the momentum needed within seconds. On the final back swing, he readied himself for the release, even though butterflies in his stomach fluttered wildly.

Once he reached the pinnacle of height, he let loose of his grip.

*Throw your head back and grab your knees tight*, he reminded himself as he soared upward, spinning through space. Three full revolutions. *Keep your eyes open and count: one, one thousand, two one thousand....*

The sensation was exhilarating, as though traveling in slow motion; one moment the darkening blue sky, and in the next, the sandbox below. Everything became topsy-turvy after his second flip, and once again entering the third.

*Now find the ground, stupid!* a voice in his head blared.

THUMP.

Steve's legs buckled slightly, absorbing the impact of a pinpoint landing mere inches from the cement barrier.

Whatever fear he had seconds earlier evaporated, replaced with a sense of grand achievement.

Amid the hooting and hollering from the gallery of friends, Jackie's screeching cut through the air.

"You did it! You did it! That was soooo bitchen!" she screamed excitedly and rushed to his side.

On tiptoes, she gave him a big hug then peered over his shoulder surreptitiously and whispered in his ear.

"Show me how to do flips when no one's around. Pul-eeeze," she pleaded. "You'll be my coach and I'll be your student. And you can teach me anything you want. *Any-thing,*" she repeated.

Taken aback, Steve gazed into her animated blue eyes, and his face flushed.

*She's only a kid ... but a darn pretty one,* he rationalized, as visions of her upside-down overruled virtuous thought.

In less than a heartbeat, his macho ego interpreted the invitation as an opportunity not to be missed.

He brushed a lock of hair from her cheek, and said with a wolfish grin, "Sweetie, you're the ginchiest. Alright, you win, but it stays a secret. Understand?"

She teasingly bit into her bottom lip and nodded.

"Dig this. I'll call you in a couple of days to let you know when we can get together. Maybe afterward we'll sneak into the ...." he never got the chance to finish the sentence.

Face aglow, she pecked him hard on the lips, then took a step back and winked at him as though some special bond had been forged between them.

With pride in her gait, Jackie sashayed back toward the gym apparatus, swishing her hips seductively while her feet playfully kicked up showers of white sand.

Awestruck, he watched her prance away, wondering what he got himself into and if he did the right thing.

A voice in his head murmured, *She's almost thirteen. That's old enough.*

After joining the group of guys, relishing their accolades, he strode over to his best friend sitting by himself on the cement curbing.

"What's that all about? Rick asked," motioning with his eyes toward Jackie.

Like a cat with feathers in its mouth, Steve shook his head, not wanting to divulge his sordid plan.

Rather than press the issue, Rick said, "Did you talk with Sue today? How are things for tomorrow night?"

"What about it?"

"September 16, you shmuck! Remember the promise at the beach last week? You and me at Sue's with Melanie."

Steve coughed out a laugh. "Just busting your balls, man. We're all set, and I guarantee it'll be a night you'll never forget."

"Does Melanie, uh, French-kiss?"

"Doesn't everybody?" Steve said. "Why are you asking?"

Gnawing on a thumbnail, Rick mumbled, "I never kissed that way because nobody ever taught me. In fact, I've never been alone with a girl."

"Jeez! I didn't know. Well, my naïve little friend, listen up. All you got to do..." Steve said, and proceeded to spend the next few minutes giving his inexperienced pal a crash course on the art of kissing.

"What if she won't open her mouth?"

"Man, are you writing a book or something?"

"No...."

"Hey! Who's the make-out king, huh? Take her lead and do what she does, and I guarantee she'll rock your world ... you lucky fuck," he added with a twinge of envy.

"Got it. I think?"

"Whatever you do, don't slobber because chicks hate that. One more thing. Don't wash her tonsils with your tongue."

A corner of Rick's mouth rose, and his hazel-brown eyes began to twinkle.

"Thanks for talking to me without making me feel like a dumb shit. Now I'm not afraid anymore," then he stood and did a crazy jig in the sand while singing aloud, "Yahoo! Going get me some poon soon. Going to get me some poon. Yabba-dabba-doo!"

Minutes later the duo mingled with the others and spent the next couple of hours working out, honing their acrobatic skills.

Jackie had long since gone home, happy her efforts to capture her dreamboat's attention finally paid off.

Suddenly, the giant outdoor floods shut off as they usually did at 11:00 P.M.

Steve's jaw dropped.

"Holy-sheep-shit!" he cried out, emphasizing each word. "Shel told me to be in by ten ... or else!"

Panicked, he scooped up his Keds and sped home barefoot.

By the time he reached his street corner, huffing and puffing, gasping for air, he saw Shel's customized '49 Merc parked at the curb in front of their building.

His throat tightened. "I'm so screwed."

# CHAPTER 6

**THE SEARCH**
September 15, 1961

THE FADING SUNLIGHT poked through the pane windows in the cluttered kitchen; colorful rays cast lined shadows over the ceramic tile countertop as remnants of the day surrendered to dusk.

Unwashed pots and dishes sat piled in the sink and the odor of cooked grease, garlic, and fried meat lingered in the air.

Seated at the table in his white skivvies with his mother in the chair next to him, Loren glanced at his wristwatch while munching on a hamburger.

Even though he hadn't eaten since breakfast, he barely tasted the blood-red patty sandwiched between the sesame-seed bun; off to the side, a hefty portion of Campbell's Pork & Beans and a scoop of homemade potato salad remained untouched.

With his stomach in knots, his mind kept drifting, antsy to go hunting, as he'd come to call it. Over the past few weekends his search for the right kids had been unsuccessful, adding to his frustration and taxing his patience.

"What's so important about the time?" Eleanor asked, spearing a kosher dill from the jar. "Got plans for the evening?"

"Kind of..." he lied, wiping a blob of ketchup from his chin. "I think I'll stop by the Purple Onion. They got two guys knocking the house down; a couple of white boys who sing like Negros. Why do you ask?"

Frowning like a spoiled child, his mother toyed with the food on her plate, mixing everything into a single heap. Then she hesitated as a boozy notion surfaced and put the fork down.

Without a trace of modesty, Eleanor impulsively tilted her chair back so he could see that her dress was hiked all the way up, exposing her tanned thighs and bright-red panties.

Loren tried not to stare - he had more urgent issues to be concerned about.

"You don't want to spend time with me," she whined, dragging the tip of the pickle across her lips suggestively while slowly spreading her legs apart. "Do you still think I'm irresistible?"

"Of course, I do." he said, dismissing her childish attempt to elicit a reaction, knowing she had already downed three highballs.

"Hell, you'll always be beautiful. Why, you're better looking than most women half your age," he stated matter-of-factly, even though he could see subtle facial changes; the fine creases around her eyes and mouth and the slight droop in her jaw line.

Tickled by his response, Eleanor sprang from her seat to make herself yet another cocktail.

As she passed in front of the last beam of waning light, the silhouette of her shapely legs through the sheer gingham fabric captured his attention.

*She's still a knockout*, he admitted. *If it wasn't for her obsession with me, some wealthy geezer might've snatched her up long ago.*

"Why don't you stay home and watch TV with me?" she said while opening the freezer and grabbing a few ice cubes from the aluminum tray, plopping them into her glass one at a time.

"Over the past month you've gone out every Friday and Saturday night and it seems like forever since we've been alone," she complained over her shoulder while filling her tumbler with two jiggers of Johnnie Walker.

Eleanor staggered back to the table and purposely brushed her thigh against his arm, trying her best to coax him.

"I give you your space," she persisted, skimming her hand across his broad hairless chest. "Tell me there's no other woman in your life. Please honey, I want to hear the words from your luscious edible lips."

"There is nobody else," he replied softly, watching her fingertips dance over his hardened nipples, sending goose bumps down his arms.

Not wanting to get into a drawn-out argument, he added, "Look, Mother, I can't explain now."

"Come on, sweetie. Let's go snuggle on the sofa and fool around under the quilt like we used to when you were younger," she slurred.

The sweet scent of her Chanel No. 5 aroused him, and he raised his head to meet her mesmerizing crystal-blue eyes.

As she teasingly raked the pleat of her dress over his nose, he could sense the heat rising from between her legs.

With arms akimbo, she smiled down at him.

"Your grandma will be at Mrs. Hinkle's

most of the night, and in case you haven't guessed, I'm hornier 'n hell. So how about it stud? Are you ready for a wild romp in the hay?"

Loren buried his brow into his mother's abdomen and pressed his mouth against her sex, sniffing her unique bouquet. He took a moment to relish the familiar aroma, then slid his hands to her waist and eased her away.

"I really want to..." he said feigning regret, "...but not tonight. Listen, I overheard Annie talking about a Pinochle marathon at her friend's house next week. Why don't we get together when she's gone? We'll have the house to ourselves all night and I promise to make it worth the wait."

"Hmph. I guess I'll have to take care of myself ... again," Eleanor mumbled, "even though it's not the same as being in bed with you."

She took a half-step back and studied her son's chiseled features.

"Be careful, my big handsome man. The city is getting to be a dangerous place with lots of crazies roaming around. Anyway, just remember to stay away from other women," she urged with a note of finality before spinning off to refresh her drink.

*You can count on that, Moth-er,* he

mused, then got up and tenderly nuzzled the side of her cheek before making a hasty retreat to the bathroom.

Having showered earlier, he washed his face to remove traces of the greasy burger and brushed his teeth while singing the Pepsodent jingle: *"You'll wonder where the yellow went when you brush your teeth with Pepsodent."*

After rinsing his mouth, he critiqued himself in the medicine cabinet mirror, flexing his biceps and flashing a killer smile, and said, "Eat your heart out, Tab Hunter."

In the bedroom, optimistic the evening would prove fruitful, he donned a clean form-fitting black tee-shirt and neatly pressed tan chinos.

He heard his mother running the water in the clawfoot cast-iron tub, softly humming to herself.

A wicked grin tugged at the corner of his mouth - *A couple of years ago, I would have fucked her brains out until she begged me to stop.*

On his way through the living room, he slid into his penny-loafers then plucked his brown corduroy jacket from the coat rack and walked out the front door.

Minutes later, he was behind the wheel and racing toward Hollywood and Highland Avenue, the crossroads of major tourist activity.

CROWDS OF SIGHTSEERS packed the sidewalks like aimless zombies. Many had their heads down, rubbernecking the Walk of Fame, ogling the names of prominent entertainers engraved on terrazzo tiles along the famed boulevard.

Outside Grauman's Chinese Theater, throngs waited to catch the re-release of The King and I, starring Yul Brenner and Deborah Kerr.

With a seating capacity of fifteen hundred, the cavernous auditorium with its ostentatious décor overwhelmed most first-time visitors. Others milled around the prestigious courtyard to gape at the concrete squares with imprints of hands and shoes of notable movie stars.

Back when Loren lived on his own for a short time, he had read that in the 1920s, showman Sid Grauman invited silent film legend Mary Pickford to the unfinished site of his new cinema designed with an Asian flair.

While they traipsed through the construction zone near the proposed box office, the drunken starlet stumbled and accidentally stepped in some freshly poured cement.

Sid gallantly suggested she autograph the embedded impression, and a tradition was born. Decades later, the markings of almost two hundred celebrities covered the forecourt.


LOREN SCANNED THE street corners as he drove by the renowned theater. Over the past year, he observed the habits of kids thumbing rides and concluded most did so in protective pairs. His dilemma: The *Chosen One* needed to be a part of the elusive duo.

At the next intersection, he journeyed south until he reached Sunset and pulled to the curb in front of Stan's Drive-In, a popular hangout for Hollywood's youth.

The carhops were pretty co-eds clothed in pink pedal-pushers that looked as though they were painted on.

Eyeballing the backside of one of the sexy servers hanging a food-tray on a car's side window, her diminutive frame caused him to flash back in time to an incident seared in his memory, replayed over and over.

**★★★★**

ELEANOR'S CLOSEST FRIEND, Amy Jacobs, called one summer morning desperately needing a babysitter and asked if Loren could help out. All he needed to do was make sure eight-year-old Johnny had his supper, supervise him when he bathed, and put him to bed by nine-thirty.

For Loren, who just turned thirteen, keeping an eye on the youngster proved to be an easy task. Mrs. Jacobs had prepared a sumptuous roasted chicken meal for the boys and stowed it in the refrigerator to be feasted upon at dinner time.

Throughout the afternoon and early evening, the kids played games of Pick-Up-Sticks, Checkers, and Monopoly. After eating and cleaning the dishes, they killed a couple of hours in the den watching television.

The antique mantel clock over the fireplace chimed at eight-thirty. It was bath time.

Settled atop the toilet seat, Loren watched with amused interest as Johnny stripped off his clothes and modestly turned his back while removing his briefs.

The moment the boy bent over to step in the tub, Loren became aware he was gawking at the lad, and an electrifying twinge stirred in his groin.

Confused by the unnatural attraction, he crossed his legs to stem his growing

85

erection, and closed his eyes. In an instant, the vision of he and his mother bathing popped into his head, her gentle hands showing him what to do.

A playful cry interrupted his sordid daydream when a floating toy shot out of the water like a rocket, landing in the corner of the room.

Loren fetched the rubber submarine and stood at the edge of the bathtub motionless, staring down at the naked boy.

Suddenly, a throaty voice in his head Murmured: *Want to have some fun?*

In a trance, the inner spirit manipulating him as though he were a puppet, Loren said to his young charge, "Do you want me to get in the tub with you?"

Johnny's eyes widened: "Yeah!" he blurted naively, welcoming the idea of a bath-time playmate.

Before undressing, Loren made him swear not to tell anyone; a secret never to be shared.

All giggles, the boy nodded and crossed his heart with a finger.

It was that night when Loren discovered what he needed in order to feel gratified.

However, as he matured, his perversion morphed into something sinister, and far more complex....

★★★★

TRAFFIC WAS LIGHT as he sped west on Sunset. The stretch of roadway between Fairfax and La Brea had no glitz, no glamorous mansions, just a four-lane artery with a mix of older stucco homes and apartment buildings set well back from the street.

Crescent Heights Boulevard marked the beginning where traditional Hollywood gave way to the current funky lifestyle, with Greenwich Village-type café's, nightclubs, burlesque parlors, and high-priced boutiques selling unique clothing and accessories to the terminally trendy.

His eyes swiveled, scanning the streets for opportunities as he continued his quest, and sighted a flock of people gathered in front of Pandora's Box, a new beatnik coffee house hosting pot-smoking bards and long-haired guitarists strumming their drug-induced ballads.

Loren despised folk music, and he hated the scraggly hippie culture even more.

Farther up the road, he spotted the famous striptease lounge aptly named, "The Body Shop." Its red and blue neon marquee featured the image of a giant woman with hips undulating back and forth.

Rolling past the vacant remnants of Ciro's nightclub, once a Mecca for the entertainment industry's elite, he eyed several girls in mini skirts walking the street clinging to grungy long-haired freaks.

He shook his head in disgust, thinking: *The days of classy Hollywood are long gone, replaced by a generation of unwashed, drugged-out degenerates.*

After passing Dino's Lodge, and then Largo, another well-known gentleman's club, he approached the city limits of Beverly Hills.

The flow of foot-traffic was anemic, so he turned south at Doheny and wound his way through upscale residential neighborhoods until he reached Santa Monica Boulevard.

Pleasantly surprised, the thoroughfare was bustling with clusters of people strolling the walkways. Many congregated on the wide median where an abandoned rapid transit railroad once ran, or as his nana called them, "Red Cars."

Off to his left, he passed the historic storefront of Barney's Beanery.

Loren had read in a magazine that John

'Barney' Anthony first opened the eclectic diner in the mid-1920s as a destination for westbound tourists traveling Route 66 toward Santa Monica Beach. Folklore had it that weary drivers could trade in their out-of-state license plates for mugs of beer and bowls of steaming hot chili.

Unable to find the right twosome, Loren cruised past PJ's nightclub and Fred Segal Menswear toward Wallichs Music City, a massive two-story building merchandizing everything from records to musical instruments. Scores of teenyboppers regularly hung around the monolith to sample their favorite 45s and newly released LPs in private sound booths.

*C'mon*, he thought, eager for action. *It's Friday night. There should be hitchhikers everywhere.*

As he neared the stoplight at Vine, something in the distance caught his eye.

Intuitively, he moved to the slow lane - a couple of youngsters with their backs to him were walking several blocks ahead.

Both appeared to be the correct height, he thought. Each with short, cropped hair, one of them seemingly overweight, the other, rather slender with a tiny butt like Johnny's.

From afar, he zeroed in on the smallest

kid, calculating his options as the Chevy
creeped ahead like a cat stalking its prey.

Then the heavy-set one turned and stuck
out a thumb toward the street.

"Yes! This might be it," Loren uttered.

He peeked over his shoulder to make
sure there were no vehicles behind him, and
all his hardware was in place on the back
seat.

His pulse quickened and his chest
tightened. The time was right, he decided,
and he tucked the switchblade under his leg
while closing in on his target.

Applying pressure to the brakes,
Loren coasted up to the unsuspecting
figures clad in black jackets and tight
jeans. At the same instant, the two young
lesbians spun around, startled.

"Aw shit! They're fucking dikes!"

In one fluid movement, he shifted his
foot to the accelerator and punched it.

"Sonofabitch!" he barked, as he
screeched away, pounding the heel of his
hand against the steering wheel. "I fucked
up!"

By the time he passed Western Avenue,
he had calmed down and realized he couldn't

afford to repeat the mistake - a lesson learned; thankful the girls didn't have the chance to see him up close. On his next outing, he would circle the block before making his approach.


IT WAS WELL after midnight when he walked in the house. Relieved his mother and Annie were asleep, he tiptoed to his room.

Disheartened over the events of the evening, he slumped onto his bed and retrieved the bound manuscript from the nightstand.

Gazing at the cover, he read the title aloud: "GOD, MAN, AND THE DEVIL, by Loren Rainsford Neestrom, August 26, 1959."

His hand trembled, recalling the day he finished writing the seventy-one-page manifesto. Its contents reflected the perverseness of his innermost beliefs and his agenda for the future. He made it a habit to re-read a few paragraphs every so often to help boost his spirits.

Flipping through the pages, he stopped at the section captioned: PHYSICAL ABSORPTION. While reviewing the chapter, an inner voice growled: *The Becoming of One*.

"The Becoming of One," Loren sighed, and a pang of sexual desire surged through him.

Horny, he hurriedly shed his clothes
and switched off the small table lamp before
climbing under the covers.

The plug-in nightlight automatically
flickered to life, and Loren stared up at
the eerie shadows while allowing his mind to
drift.

Soon, his eyes closed, and bizarre
images crept into his thoughts - a handsome
incubus, a likeness of himself, infiltrated
his fantasy world; one moment an apparition
of Eleanor stroking him, and in the next,
little Johnny taking her place.

Erotic sensations pulsated through him
and he began to masturbate.

In his dreamlike state, he was in a
steamy shower, but not alone. Soapy hands
caressed his muscular body, and his lips
were enmeshed with a faceless lover, their
tongues entwined in a feverish dance.

Suddenly, he was chomping into soft
fleshy tissue and warm fluid spurted in his
mouth. Fingernails clawed in desperation at
his shoulders and a blood-curdling scream
echoed in his head.

Loren's orgasm left him well sated as
he sank into a deep deep slumber.

# CHAPTER 7

**THE ARGUMENT**
September 16, 1961
5:00 PM

"YOU'RE PUNISHED!" Shel bellowed, his voice hammering Steve's ears all the way from the living room. "You screwed up so now you got to pay the piper."

With a worried glance at Rick standing in the bedroom doorway, Steve yelled back defiantly knowing his brother wasn't in the mood to argue.

"What do you mean?"

"Obviously, you didn't take me seriously last night when I told you to be home from the playground by ten o'clock. Remember me saying, 'Not ten-thirty, not ten-fifteen'? But no, you figured, fuck him and his silly rules, didn't you?"

Not hearing a response, his beer-fueled anger flared.

Shel threw his cards face-down on the poker table, and said to his buddies, Howard and Harry, "Watch this. All hell's going to break lose," then he got up and stormed down the long hallway of their spacious two-bedroom apartment.

Barging into the room, Shel shoved Rick out of the way and glared at his young charge sitting on the edge of the bed.

"Not only did you piss me off by breaking curfew," continuing his rant up close and personal, "but Harry said he spotted you and Jeff hitchhiking from school the other day, even though mom gave you bus fare for the week."

"Well, I was short on cash."

"How many times have I told you not to hitchhike! And what the hell did you do with the money? Buy smokes and junk food?"

"Come on man," Steve whined, deftly changing the subject. "Tonight's super important. We're supposed to be at Sue's because her parents are going out partying ... and you know what that means," he added with a Groucho Marx eyebrow lift.

Shel took a couple of menacing steps forward but stopped short.

With hands on his hips, his face a blustery-red, he barked: "Listen to me good, jerkoff. I've been mentoring you for your mother's sake who somehow believes you'll outgrow your arrogance."

"I know that."

"Really? Up 'til now, you've been able to con our mother on a regular basis. Just because her and dad are deaf mutes, doesn't mean they're stupid people. Ever since their divorce, she depends on you to interpret for her when needed, and all she asks of you is to do small chores around the house while she's at work."

"Wait a minute. I..."

"Can it buster! You can't bullshit a bullshitter. Every lame excuse you come up with, I've used. If you're going to justify your fuck-ups, be creative, you might score some points."

"But..."

"Shut up, I'm not done talking!" Shel railed. "I'm six years older and a hell-of-a-lot wiser. For the longest time I've tried my best to keep you on the straight and narrow. *We* don't ask for much, but there are certain standards you need to live by. Break 'em and I kick your butt. It's as simple as that. Not like the times when mom stopped me from whipping your sorry ass."

With a defeated dip of his head, Steve remembered all too well the days following his brother's release from Juvenile Hall.

**★★★★**

SHORTLY AFTER TURNING seventeen, Shel and his delinquent friends were apprehended sneaking into the Culver City Police impound lot to steal auto parts.

Incarcerated for six months at Lincoln Heights Detention Center, a toxic environment known for breeding future felons, he had plenty of free time to think about his errant life.

With sage counseling from his Uncle Dan, it was at that point when he decided not to let his little brother follow the same misguided path, even though Steve had already showed signs of delinquency — he had just turned twelve and was busted operating a bicycle chop-shop out of their garage.

When released from juvy, Shel wasted no time convincing his mother, Sarah Bell, to turn over the reins tutoring his mischievous brother.

She consented with one caveat: no corporal punishment. Reluctantly, he agreed, even though he believed his cocky coming-of-age sibling deserved an ass whooping now and then to teach him the difference between right from wrong.

**★★★★**

STEVE'S HEART SANK - according to plan, by the end of the evening, he and steady his girlfriend would no longer be virgins, their

youthful passion for one another forever
cemented.

"Aw c'mon bro. Remember the stuff we
talked about yesterday. We'll, this is the
night!"

"Tough shit. The answer's still no!"
Shel growled. "You should've thought about
that instead of coming home an hour late.

"I forgot my watch."

"Like hell you did! You're the one who
screwed up, not me. So now I'm holding you
accountable for your actions. Call it a
lesson learned because it'll come in handy
if you ever grow up to be a responsible
adult rather than a self-absorbed punk."

Seeing his evening going up in flames,
Steve tried to protest, but Rick, quick off
the mark with his mouth, beat him to the
punch.

"Hey, lighten up, man!" he bellyached.
"We got to go because Sue fixed me up with
Melanie! This is a chance of a lifetime for
me to be with a hot babe, so don't be such a
grumpy dick."

Steve cringed.

"Oh yeah?" said Shel, turning to Rick,
towering over him by a foot and twice his
weight. "Well, you're grounded too,

motherfucker!" his rejoinder short and
sweet.

"Hey! You can't do that!"

For a brief moment Shel contemplated
giving the smart-ass a wicked backhand but
thought better and wheeled away in a huff,
returning to the card game and his half-
empty can of Pabst Blue Ribbon.

"Want me to send in the *Beast*?" he
hollered after taking his seat at the table.

Wide-eyed, the boys grimaced - they did
not want the Beast to intervene.

Howard Kravitz was an exceptionally
large man with a short fuse. Topping out at
six foot six and weighing well over three-
hundred fifty pounds, he was graced with the
physique of a bodybuilder; shoulders wide as
an Amana refrigerator and biceps the size of
cantaloupes. With simian features, a sloped
brow and deep-set hooded eyes, he was an
imposing behemoth to behold.

Treated like members of the Bell
household, Howard and Harry Goldman were
Shel's closest pals, each with personalities
different as night and day - Harry's
demeanor, *'Make love, not war'*. Howard, on
the other hand, preferred making war.


RICK STARED DOWN at his high-top Keds,

realizing the opportunity to be with his
dream girl had slipped through his grasp,
and with it, the experience of swapping spit
with one of the hottest girls at Fairfax
High.

"Guess you'll have to call you-know-
who," he sighed. "She's not going be a happy
camper.

Tight-lipped, Steve nodded, and put his
finger to his lips and whispered, "Stay put.
I'll be right back."

He peeked out the bedroom door, then
tip-toed to the kitchen where he could
eavesdrop on *The Three Musketeers*, a moniker
given his brother and two life-long pals.

Spying on them while the trio discussed
plans for the evening, he quietly picked up
the wall-phone and dialed.

A breathless voice came on the line.
"Hello?"

With his hand cupping the mouthpiece,
he said, "We can't come over. I got put on
restriction."

"Whaaat?" Sue screeched, forcing him to
pull the receiver from his ear. "You can't
do this! Mel's here and my parents are
rolling out of the driveway. We've got tons
of food and I even stole vodka from daddy's
bar. The house is ours all-night-long," she

moaned, emphasizing the last three words.

"Honey, I..."

"What the hell did you do this time?" she said flatly, cutting him off.

He tried to explain but she kept interrupting. All he could do was answer, "uh huh," trying to keep his end of the conversation short, primarily relegated to "Yes's" and "No's."

"Wouldn't you like to see me naked?" she teased. "Find a way to get over here and I'll let you do everything you ever wanted to do. And I swear I won't stop you. Not this time."

Erotic images raced through his head, clouding rational thought. "Call you back soon," he said, and hung up.

STEVE FOUND RICK sitting on the front porch step, hands propped under his chin, sulking. The first words out of his mouth: "What's the thing you're not sharing with me?"

"I promise I'll tell you later, Steve replied, firing up a Marlboro and taking a spot next to his nosy cohort.

"Her parents are just leaving," he said, and then took a long drag of his

cigarette and blew out a perfect set of
smoke rings. "The frig is stocked with
goodies and a pitcher of screwdrivers is
waiting for us. Now here's what we're going
to do...."

Rick eyed his buddy with reserved
optimism.

"The guys were talking about going to
either Pink's or Tommy's on Alvarado for a
bite. Afterwards, they'll hit a party in
Eagle Rock or Hollywood Hills. So, when they
split, we're out of here."

"Do you realize if Shel finds out,
he'll pound your ass from here to Kingdom
Come."

Steve shot him a concerned look, then
tossed his half-smoked cigarette into the
flowerbed of roses and padded back to the
kitchen to call Sue.

She answered the phone before the first
ringtone ended. "This better be good news."

"Stop yakking," he interrupted with a
sense of urgency. "We'll be at your place
soon as my brother leaves and we can thumb a
ride. And don't forget what you said,
'Anything I want,'" then he eased the
handset down with a smile and went back
outside.

The boys shared a few more smokes on

the stoop, anxiously waiting for a telltale sign The Musketeer's were getting ready to leave.

The sound from the stereo bled through the open French windows, pumping out 45s by Jerry Lee Lewis, Elvis, and The Platters. In the background, they heard Harry's plaintive howl Howard cheated again.

After what seemed like an eternity, the music stopped, and the trio of young men barged out the front door and piled into Howard's powder-blue super-charged '57 Ford.

Before roaring off, Shel stuck his head out the passenger window and shouted, "Don't sneak out or you're dead meat, mister!" That's when Howard floored the Blue Monster and the beefy rear slicks spun in place against the rough asphalt.

With tires squealing and plumes of burnt rubber spewing from the undercarriage, the hotrod lurched forward like a rocket, producing a trail of black tire marks halfway up the block.

Steve gazed at the car as it gradually disappeared from view.

"Screw him! What the hell does he know?" Then he turned to Rick and said, "Tonight's going to be so fucking memorable for both of us."

# CHAPTER 8

## A LOVER'S QUARREL

STEVE SHOWERED QUICKLY, then stepped into a clean pair of jeans and long-sleeve powder blue button-down oxford shirt. After glimpsing at himself in the mirror, he slipped into his sneakers and snatched his nylon bomber-jacket before flying out the front door with Rick in tow.

In the gathering dusk, ominous storm clouds had formed in the west over the Pacific, but the duo paid little heed while jogging up Wooster Street toward the bustling intersection of Pico and Robertson.

Saturday evening traffic was heavy so getting a couple of rides didn't take long; the last one dropping them off at the Jewish Community Center on Olympic, a couple of blocks from their destination.

In front of Sue's sprawling ranch-style house, Rick comically sniffed his armpits, and then ran a comb through his hair adequately peppered with Brylcreem, smoothing his mop of curly locks in place.

With an impish smirk, he stuck out his tongue, darting it like a snake sensing its prey. "I've been practicing all day," he boasted.

Put off by the childish antic, Steve took a long puff of his cigarette, and said, "Quit screwing around mo-ron. People will think we're fags swapping spit."

Rick's brow went up and he made a what-the-hell-did-I-do-wrong gesture with his hands.

It took him a few seconds to realize what irked his uptight pal but couldn't resist the temptation to push it further.

"Thay thweetie," he lisped, batting his eyes theatrically and flipping out a limp wrist. "I'm not good enough for you, Studley?"

Steve scowled and his nostrils flared.

Satisfied that he pissed-off his cocky sidekick, Rick pulled a pack of Sen-Sens from his pocket and tossed a couple of the tiny black, licorice-flavored pieces in his mouth.

"Well, I guess now's the time for me to grow a pair," he said, and then walked up the stoop, squared his shoulders and rang the doorbell.

THE GIRLS APPEARED at the threshold

and the sight took Steve's breath away.

Clad in skin-tight black capris with matching cashmere vee-neck sweater, Sue's sun-bleached platinum-blond hair accentuated a tanned pixie-like face with tantalizing lips and a sprinkling of freckles across the bridge of a turned-up nose.

He took in every inch of her well-toned body with lustful anticipation, and then sneakily shifted his gaze to Melanie.

Several inches taller than Sue and lithe as a runway model, she exuded an aura of sexual vitality. Decked out in a cropped blue halter top and racy white hip-huggers seated well below her waistline, she did a lazy pirouette, pausing long enough to display picture-perfect ass that would make a Playboy model turn green with envy.

For a fleeting moment she peeked over her shoulder and locked eyes with Steve.

A twinge of excitement rippled through him as he visually undressed her, only to be interrupted by the sound of his overly possessive girlfriend.

"Ahem," Sue cleared her throat loudly while glaring at Steve. "You sure took your time getting here," she huffed. "Mel, maybe you should you take Rick to the family room and play some of my new albums. And don't forget about the food and pitcher of screwdrivers in the fridge."

With the subtlety of a fox in a hen
house, she added, "I hope you all will
excuse us, but we're going to chat in
private for a while," then she hooked Steve
by the elbow and scurried him to her
bedroom.


THE TIFFANY LAMP on the baroque oak
nightstand barely illuminated the cluttered
room, casting muted rays against paisley-
papered walls.

An oversized brown teddy-bear sat atop
a white-lace bedspread, neatly surrounded by
dozens of smaller stuffed animals – Steve
recalled her squeal of delight after he won
it from one of the concessions stands at
Pacific Ocean Park. That was the night she
let him feel her up for the first time.

Sue closed the door and spun around to
embrace him.

He drew her in and pressed his body
against hers, and in no time, their lips met
and their tongues danced with passion.

From the next room, the faint sound of
Rosie and the Originals singing Angel Baby
could be heard on the stereo.

Wrapped in each other's arms, they
swayed to the melody while Sue whispered the

words: "When you are near me, my heart skips a beat. I can hardly stand on, my own two feet...."

The tantalizing fragrance of her perfume wafted over him as their bodies moved in sync.

Filled with pent-up desire, his arousal mounted, and soon the notion of extended foreplay flew out the window.

He slipped a hand under her sweater and deftly unhooked her bra in one swift move.

She shuddered and her breathing quickened while his fingers glided over her ample breasts, caressing them delicately at first, enjoying the erotic sensation for several torrid minutes.

*God, she has great tits*, Steve thought.

The heated moments lingered, and soon his fingers slithered lower, floating ever so softly across her flat tummy.

When he tried to unfasten the front of her pants, she stopped him with a hand and mumbled in his ear, "You love me don't you?"

"Always," he said while nibbling the side of her neck, the saltiness of her perspiration exciting him on even more.

"Are you sure you want to do this?

Maybe we shouldn't...."

"Shh," he cooed - *she always says the same thing*, he reflected. It had taken him time to understand her dilemma; years of rigid parental indoctrination forced her to guard her virginity as though she were wearing a chastity belt, yet another part of her longed to experience the heat of sex.

Over the past several months, he had made a conscientious effort to be respectful and not go beyond her limits; restricting him to long make-out sessions, dry humping and copping a feel now and then - she never allowed him to touch her sweet spot.

*But not tonight*, he affirmed: the scent of her skin, the taste of her lips, her body urging him hungrily — he couldn't stop now if he wanted to. He thought, *If Junior had vocal cords, he'd be screaming, 'Hurry up and let me out of here 'cause the pump is primed'*.

As they continued to kiss passionately, he slyly undid the top clasp of her capris and gingerly tugged at the zipper pull-tab, lowering it one jagged notch at a time.

With just enough room to maneuver, his fingers slid beneath her silk panties and probed as though they had a mind of their own.

"Sweetheart, slow down. I'm scared,"

she said. "I want you but...."

"You talk too much," he murmured.

His hand slithered downward until his fingertips reached the coarseness of her pubic hair. *Easy now. Only another inch or two....*

"No!" she suddenly cried out," pushing him away and shaking her head. Her eyes welled, "I'm sorry baby, I can't. No matter how much I want you."

"Whaaa!" Steve stammered as the words sank in. *She promised this was to be our night. And if I get caught for sneaking out, I'm screwed twice. All because of her.*

"That's it!" he barked. "I've had it."

"Honey, don't be mad. I know how you're feeling but I can't help it. You still love me, don't you?" she whined.

Tight-lipped, he gazed at the doorway while muted laughter bled through the wall from the other room against the backdrop of Johnnie Mathis crooning, *Chances Are.*

"Hey, you're not listening to me."

"No, I'm not."

"Would you rather have someone with a wild reputation like Melanie, or a girl who you'd respect?"

Months of broken promises rose to the surface and his temper flared.

"Well at least she's not a prick teaser," he replied, spitting the words out. "To tell you the truth, I wouldn't mind trading places with Rick right now."

Sue's jaw dropped.

"Far as I'm concerned...," pointing a finger at her, "...it's Endsville for us. No more games, and no more lame excuses."

Steve unclasped the clunky silver ID bracelet from his wrist and watched it fall to the cushy white shag carpet. "There! Now we're not going steady anymore."

In a fit of escalating anger, he grabbed the large teddy bear from the bed and shoved it against her chest.

"Here, hump this when you get lonely," he said red-faced, then stormed out of the room before she could react.

In the dimly lit den, he spotted his buddy on the leather sofa with Melanie, an arm draped over her shoulder, the other halfway up her blouse.

Startled, Rick's head popped up: "What the f—? What's going on?"

"I'm out of here," Steve said, slipping into his jacket while heading toward the foyer. "You can tell my ex-girlfriend to fuck around with someone else. I'm done with her forever!"

"Man, don't say that," Rick pleaded, jumping to his feet and tucking in his shirttails. "We're having a hellofa time here. Mel was just going to show me a new Latin dance. It's called the Horizontal Mambo."

Steve froze mid-step, then turned and glared - he was in no mood for wisecracks.

Hastily fastening her bra, Melanie flashed him a sorrowful look and backed out of Rick's field-of-view, then puckered a kiss and mouthed the words, "Call me tomorrow night."

Incensed, Steve strode out the front door, slamming it shut behind him.

# CHAPTER 9

## RIDE TO FATE

HALFWAY UP THE block: "Hold on Kemosabe! Slow down," Rick gasped as he caught up with his rabid friend.

Between breaths, he puffed, "Now what the fuck ... was that... all about?"

Instead of answering, Steve pointed to the massive thunderheads rapidly closing in from the west, not quite ready to reveal the cause of his hasty exit.

"We're in for some nasty weather," he said. "Hope it won't take us long to get home."

The boys walked in silence for a bit, each with their own thoughts how the evening turned out.

"Been a fucked-up night," Steve finally uttered, fishing a Marlboro from his pack. He offered one to Rick, and they huddled together against the breeze after he flicked open his trusty Zippo with a snap of his fingers, lighting both smokes at the same time.

"Sorry for spoiling your fun because I know what it meant to you."

"Hey man, I'm your best bud. Where you go, I go!"

BY THE TIME they reached the main drag it began to drizzle, and Steve had calmed down enough to disclose what took place in the bedroom.

"No shit?" Rick chuckled. "I thought you took Tony to Tuna Town a long time ago. Hell, with a body like Sue's, you got to have the patience of a saint."

"Yeah, dumb little me. What I couldn't tell you before is that we planned this for weeks. On the phone this afternoon, she promised to let me do anything I wanted. Can you dig how pumped up I was?"

He stopped to take another long draw off the cigarette and continued his tale of woe.

"In her room, we were all hot and bothered from making out and me playing with her boobs. Then, after unzipping her pants, ready drop her drawers, she changed her mind. So, I got pissed, said some things I shouldn't have, and gave her back my ID bracelet. Now we're finished."

After a few awkward moments, Rick

nodded sympathetically and decided to spill the beans about Melanie.

"When I put my lips to hers, she stuck her tongue in my mouth just like you said. The feeling was un-fucking unbelievable!"

Walking side-by-side, Steve listened with a mixture of amusement and envy, wondering what happened next.

"I did everything you told me and I think she was digging it. Then she put her hand on my leg and started rubbing, going higher and higher," he gushed, demonstrating the movement up his thigh.

"Man-oh-man, I had such a boner! But when she unhooked her bra and let me feel her tits, I thought I died and went to heaven! They were sooooo soft. I never felt anything like it. Anyway, it got to where I couldn't hold back and I ... uh ..."

Impatient, Steve interrupted: "Out with it, putz!"

"All right. All right. I'm embarrassed, that's all," Rick said, smashing his cigarette on the concrete with the heel of his shoe and kicking the butt to the gutter. "I shot my wad in my underwear. Satisfied?"

Unable to control himself, Steve dropped to his knees on the damp concrete and laughed until his gut ached, all the while his naive compadre standing over him with his arms out and palms up, shouting, "What? What?"


AT THE INTERSECTION of Fairfax and Olympic, Steve took the first turn hitchhiking.

A sudden crack of lightning illuminated the sky, and the ensuing rumble of thunder shook the ground. Seconds later the mist turned into sporadic drops, and Rick sought shelter under the canvas awning of a nearby real estate office.

With thumb outstretched, Steve hoped to catch a ride before the tempest hit full force.

Before long, he was taken off guard by a blaring Klaxon - not a typical car horn, but more of a piercing, *A-OOO-GAH, A-OOO-GAH.*

His jaw dropped and he did a double-take when the customized Cadillac Eldorado Brougham coasted to a stop in front of him.

The sleek luxury sedan had been painted pearlescent white that glistened like a million stars under the streetlights, and in place of the iconic Cadillac emblem on the front, a magnificent set of steer horns were mounted on the hood.

When Steve opened the car door, he was bowled over by a cloud of pungent cigar smoke. *Oh shit, Rick will hate this. With his weak stomach he'll probably barf.*

"Where y'all headed, boy?" the rotund man asked with a heavy southern drawl.

"My buddy and I need a lift to Robertson Boulevard. Are you going that far?"

"No problem son," he replied. "I'm a-headin' to Santa Monica and have to pass by there. Jump on in."

The driver reminded Steve of what a stereotypical oil tycoon from Texas should look like: Millionaire mogul clad in a custom thousand-dollar hand-tailored suit, wearing a matching beige Stetson and a pair of Lucchese ostrich boots; him stretched way back in the seat with his huge beer belly brushing the bottom of the steering wheel while gnawing on a fat Corona.

Steve's instincts told him the man appeared harmless, so he whistled out to Rick they had a ride and slid onto the softest leather he had ever felt.

Rick followed suit, and he too was greeted by the sharp cigar odor after opening the back door, only his reaction was unexpected. His face screwed up and his nostrils flared: "Holy crap ... it stinks in here!"

*Diplomacy was not one of Rick's finer
qualities*, Steve mused - his immature
blabbermouth had gotten them in trouble many
times. *Ahh, but tonight, I nailed him. The
funky stench will definitely make him puke.*

Shrugging his shoulders, he eyed the
sizable gent behind the wheel apologetically
and raised his brow as if to say, *Sorry, but
my partner lacks tact.*

The wily old Texan seemed to pick up on
the humor and winked his understanding, then
took a big puff and blew a plume of gray
toward the rear seat.

Steve held back the urge to burst out
laughing and stared out the side window as
the car surged away, relishing the irony of
it all.

With a chuckle, the man said over his
shoulder, "Better get used to the smell
'cause it's a gitt'n mighty wet out there
and the windows are a-goin' all the way up."

Rick's eyes widened and asked if he
could lower the window an inch or so, his
voice suddenly sounding humbled and meek.

Pulling the soggy-tipped stogie from
his mouth, the man let out a thunderous roar
that caused a band of ash to fall on his
lap.

"Not a chance, boy. Don't want to ruin the imported leather upholstery. Do we?"

VISIBILITY RAPIDLY DETERIORATED on their westward trek. Intermittent showers soon erupted into a torrential downpour and the streets began to flood.

Twenty minutes later they stopped curbside at the corner of Robertson and Olympic.

Rick flew out the door, sucking in gulps of air, coughing and sputtering his displeasure - he didn't care if it was pouring cats and dogs, preferring mouthfuls of water rather than breathing in noxious fumes.

After thanking the driver, Steve got out and watched the sleek sedan disappear into the curtain of rain.

"You did that to me on purpose!" Rick shouted. "I know you did, because you know how much I hate the stink of cigars."

"What the hell are you bitching about? I got us here in a tricked-out Eldo, didn't I? All we need now is to catch a ride south so let's jam across the street before we have to swim home."

With the fierce torrent pelting the

duo, they sloshed toward the bright overhead
lights of the Chevron station, barely
noticing the familiar historical marker:
*WELCOME TO BEVERLY HILLS.*

# CHAPTER 10

**THE HUNT**

TEMPORARILY SATED, LOREN slowly arose from the tattered couch and stood on wobbly legs. The oak floor beneath him creaked as he carefully made his way to the bathroom, shutting the door behind him.

Silently, he cleaned his perspiration-soaked body with a damp washrag — first his face, armpits, and then his limp appendage, still oozing seminal fluid.

Raking his fingers through his tousled hair, he gazed intently at the medicine cabinet mirror - the striking image with riveting crystal-blue eyes staring back told him to get out of the house before Mother woke up wanting another go-around.

"Destiny calls," he murmured, and the rabid beasts from within began to stir. *Time to go hunting*, they echoed in unison.

Naked, he padded back to the darkened living room in search for his clothes.

Traces of light flickered from the television set with the volume turned down, casting ghostly shadows on Eleanor sprawled atop the sofa, snoring.

*The years have been good to her*, he
thought, recalling the previous night and
how desperate she'd been about having sex.

But tonight, with Annie unexpectedly
out for the evening, she had managed to
trigger a hot button and they made love
until she screamed in submission, begging
him to stop the pain.

Watching Eleanor's full breasts rise
and fall with each breath, he scrutinized
her beautiful body - a body he knew
intimately, every nook and cranny.

Suddenly his mind went blank.

In the fog, often guided by malevolent
forces frequenting his thoughts, his eyes
shifted to her slender neck, imagining how
easy it would be to wrap a meaty paw around
it and squeeze the life out of her perverted
soul.

Spellbound, he reached for her throat.

*STOP!* hollered one of the familiar
voices in his head.

Startled by the impulsive urge to
strangle the woman he just ravaged, he
stepped back. *What's happening to me?*

Another alter-ego, far more feral

than the others, chimed in: *DO IT! THE BITCH DESERVES TO DIE. KILL HER!*

With palms cupped over his ears, Loren shook his head like a dog shedding water, trying to silence the cacophony assaulting his senses.

After several deep breaths, his panic attack slowly ebbed, and he removed his hands - the only sound to be heard was that of Eleanor purring like a contented cat.

"Goodbye Mother," he whispered, and turned off the TV.

Blessed with the ability to see exceptionally well in the dark, he retrieved his pants and loafers off the floor and tiptoed to the kitchen.

Hurriedly, he slipped into his trousers, and then realized his tee-shirt and socks were missing - most likely buried somewhere beneath his mother.

"Aw shit," he grumbled. To get a fresh set of clothes, he'd have to pass through the room and didn't want to take the chance of waking her.

*To hell with it. I'm out of here*. Bare-chested, he snatched his denim jacket from the back of the dinette chair and ducked out the side door, shoes in hand.

Outside the apartment, he donned his coat and slipped into his loafers, then glanced up at the sky blanketed with ominous clouds and sniffed the cool night air.

"Smells sweet. Just like Mother's pussy," he sighed.

With spring in his gait at the start, by the time he reached the car, his mood had soured.

Feeling used again, he wondered why he always caved to her bizarre needs.

Society called it incest, but throughout his formative years she taught him that in centuries past, royalty considered it honorable and natural; a way to keep bloodlines intact.

The never-ending indoctrination intensified during his teen years, and even now, he remained baffled how she sexually dominated him; touch the right spot at the right time and he flicked on like a light switch, unable to stop until her aberrant pleasures were fulfilled.

Once again, the haunting vision of a pubescent lad flashed in his thoughts. The ever-frequent fantasy had become his driving force, keeping him focused on what he wanted. What he desperately craved.

LOREN STARTED THE engine and listened to the throaty sound of eight cylinders idling, goosing the gas pedal a couple of times before shifting into gear and edging out of the parking slot.

A quick stop at the Union 76 to top off the Chevy's tank and he was southbound on Vermont by eight-thirty.

On a hunch, he decided to drive to Culver City, and turned right at Wilshire.

While cruising the renowned business corridor, he paid little attention to the glamorous landmarks: the stately Ambassador Hotel and Coconut Grove; across the street, the Brown Derby, a prominent dining venue for Hollywood's elite.

After passing La Cienega, he stopped in front of Dolores' Drive-In, a hang-out for local teens.

He scoped out the crowd, seeking the right ones; height, weight, age, and appearance - it was all calculated in the plan. Minutes later he pulled away from the curb. *Too old*, he thought.

Focused on his mission while driving westbound on Wilshire, silver slivers crossed the headlight beams as it began to drizzle.

Loren switched on the wipers, and he

cut south at Robertson on a route that would take him to the A & W Root Beer on Sepulveda.

Then the unthinkable happened; the sky opened like a faucet and the ensuing deluge pummeled the car. In seconds, the roadway turned slick and heavy drops bounced off the hood.

"Fuck! Fuck! Fuck! This is going to screw up everything," he cursed, and flipped the wiper control to MAX.

A quarter of a mile from Olympic, he spotted the faint silhouette of a person hunched over at the corner by the Chevron, arm waving in the air. *A hitchhiker?*

Like a predator tracking its prey, Loren tensed and peeked over his shoulder - no cars behind him, only the yellow glare of streetlamps and their distorted reflections off on the flooded blacktop.

As he neared the signal, the floodlights from the service station illuminated the figure standing curbside.

*It's a kid! And a young one at that.*

Then the boy spun on his heels and motioned to someone under the brightly lit canopy.

"Hot damn! There's two of them," Loren

said excitedly. "I can't fucking believe it!"

With his foot off the gas, he killed the headlights and eyed the two while slowly coasting past them, mentally checking off preferences.

*There! The cute one with the pompadour by the pumps. Can't be more than twelve or thirteen. He's perfect!*

Mid-way through the intersection, he glimpsed at the rear view and caught sight of the hitchhiker jumping up and down in the middle of the road, flipping him the bird.

*Well, I can assure you the little shit'll regret that,"* growled a virulent inner-voice.

Cognizant of the episode with the lesbians from the night before, he hung a right at the first street and doubled back through the tree-lined upscale neighborhood.

The unrelenting maelstrom pounded the car as it plowed through the torrents, sending waves of murky gutter-water across the windshield. It didn't matter to Loren – he finally found the *Chosen One*.

# CHAPTER 11

## THE CONNECTION

*SERENDIPITY, YOU LUCKY* sonofabitch, whispered a voice in Loren's head as he circled the block.

A burst of euphoria swept through him, marveling at the fortuitous series of events placing the targets within reach – being in the right place at the precise moment, with the perfect pair of unsuspecting boys.

Even though the rain pelted the windshield, he could see the hitchhiker standing at the corner with a thumb out.

Loren took in a deep breath, and said, "It's showtime."

The car slowed to 15 mph, and with everything secured in place, he veered to the curb, easing to a stop in front of the knucklehead who flipped him the bird.

The brazen boy rapped on the window, then opened the door and fearlessly poked his head inside. In seconds, water from his rain-soaked jacket dribbled over the tuck and roll upholstery, and Loren winced before offering up a forced Hollywood smile.

"Where you headed?" he asked.

"My friend and I need a lift to Airdrome," said the boy.

"No problem. I'm going to Culver City so get your buddy and hop in," knowing all that mattered was getting the *special* one seated next to him on the front seat.

The youngster backed out and barked to his pal under the canopy of the Chevron Station.

Loren thought he shouted the name, 'Steve.' *Hmm? I think I'll call him Steven. He might not like it, but tough shit.*

For what seemed like an eternity, he waited to see how his cards would play out; hoping luck was still with him.

With the engine purring in a low idle, the whooshing of the wipers had a mesmerizing effect, casting him into a daydream of a large spider perched at the edge of its web, ready to pounce on trapped prey.

The predatory image shattered at the sound of the hitchhiker yelling the word, "Shotgun," and his friend running toward the car answering, "Rick. You're such an asshole!"

"Rick-the-prick," Loren uttered with

an evil smirk, "A fitting name for the piece of garbage who tossed me the bone. He has no idea what's in store for him."

One of the inner voices chimed in: *Everything depends on who gets in first. It has to be the cute kid. If not, we'll be forced to give them a ride to wherever the fuck Airdrome is and call it a night.*

The door opened unexpectedly and the Chosen One stuck his head inside.

Startled, Loren stammered for words: "Oh! Uh ... My name's Loren. And welcome to my web."

The boy paused for the briefest of moments, and then without a word, tried to flip the backrest to climb in.

"Hey! You can't sit there! Loren panicked. "Both of you need to be up front with me 'cause I've got important stuff on the back seat that can't be disturbed."

The lad scowled and started to say something, then stopped short and got out, leaving the door slightly ajar.

A trickle of perspiration rolled down the side of Loren's neck as tortuous seconds dragged by while the kids argued in the rain.

Suddenly the door flew open, and a

laughing Rick-the-Prick was shoving the
Chosen One headfirst onto the front seat.


*GAME, SET AND MATCH*, hooted one of
Loren's inner-voices. *With the rigged door
closed, the trap is set*, said another.

After crossing Olympic heading south on
Robertson, bolts of energy began to course
through Loren like shards of lightning;
every cell in his body seemingly electrified
while he navigated the flooded four-lane
artery.

Soon he started to hallucinate and
reflections from the storefronts tweaked
into strange shapes and wavy lines, creating
the illusion of being transported into Van
Gogh's Starry Night; all the scenes
distorted, morphing into new objects. Even
the asphalt rippled as raindrops leaped from
the pavement in a ritualistic dance.

The pace of bizarre images continued to
gain momentum as Loren's thoughts spiraled
out of control.

Amid the cacophony assaulting his
senses, a likeness of his mother suddenly
popped into his head. Her beautiful smile
slowly twisted into a feral snarl like that
of a rabid dog displaying fangs with strings
of goo dripping from its gaping maw.

The impression was so vivid Loren

almost gasped aloud and forced himself to blink several times to help clear the horrifying visions.

Tiny beads of sweat had formed on his forehead and he wanted to swipe at them but was too paralyzed to take his hands off the wheel, almost afraid to breathe.

To avoid an outright panic attack, he whispered a mantra from a chapter in his manifesto: "Soon there will be tranquility and conflation ...," repeating the chant, over and over.

*The Becoming of One*, he fantasized; his defining moment, a re-birth of the person who endured years of torment and a life of perverted manipulation at the hands of a deranged mother. That man would be dead, and like a butterfly escaping its cocoon, he too would emerge as a new entity. The story was already written in his head. All he had to do was act it out.

The mere mention of the soothing words helped to restore his wits, snapping him back to the present.

Now acutely aware of his surroundings, he furtively glanced at his passengers preoccupied with the wood block on the dashboard.

*Hmm? What are the chances of finding two kids hitchhiking late at night during a thunderstorm? And then wind up with the Chosen One sitting next to me?*

Filled with anticipation, he felt as though he had just cheated the odds.


THEY SOON APPROACHED Pico, and as he slowed down for the red traffic light, the boy next to him broke the palpable unease.

"Mister, you can let us off here."

Loren's jaw dropped as the words soaked in. *They want to get out? No fucking way! Not now. Not ever!*

Quickly scanning his surroundings, he re-calculated - few cars on the road and none behind him as the Chevy rolled to a gradual stop.

On the other side of the boulevard, he eyeballed a less conspicuous area away from possible detection from any passing motorists.

"Why don't I drop you guys off across the street? It'll be safer."

Without waiting for an answer, he drove through the flooded intersection when the signal turned green and zeroed in on the dark stretch sandwiched between two burned-out streetlamps.

Rainwater in the gutter sprayed over the sidewalk like a tsunami as the tires brushed the curb before the Chevy came to rest.

Sliding the gearshift into neutral, he casually lowered his left arm to the trigger device, waiting for the right moment.

Out of the corner of his eye he caught sight of Rick-the-prick fumbling with the inoperable door handle. The second the kid leaned back flush against the seat, Loren squeezed the jerry-rigged handbrake.

BANG!

A sharp crack echoed through the cabin and the boy riding shotgun screamed, "Owwww! My back! I think I've been shot."

# CHAPTER 12

## THE RIDE CONTINUES

STARTLED BY THE loud noise, Steve's first instinct was a truck backfired, even though none passed by. At the same instant, hearing his best friend yell, "...I think I've been shot," only heightened the confusion.

A quick glance at the pained expression etched on Rick's face and he knew he wasn't clowning around.

*But how could he have been shot? Is someone hiding on the floor in the back?* he wondered, recalling the precautionary peek before getting into the car.

In those first turbulent seconds, nothing made sense.

"Get down out of firing range!" the handsome stranger behind the wheel hollered. "Hurry!"

*What the hell?* Steve reeled, trying to sort things out. *What does he mean, '...out of firing range'? No glass shattered from a bullet bursting through the back window.*

He glimpsed once more at his pal slumped against the door at an awkward angle and suddenly realized something far more sinister was unfolding.

CLICK!

Steve's eyes widened at the unmistakable sound of a switchblade flicking open, but when it materialized out of the murky shadows and was pressed against his throat, he nearly peed in his pants.

The man leaned in close and spoke in a tone laced with evil intent: "Kid, I've killed before and won't hesitate to do it again." After a brief pause, as if to let the threat sink in, he added, "So do as you're told, and I might let you live."

From the moment Steve heard the chilling words, "I've killed before...," his carefree life screeched to a halt, frozen in time. There was no day. No night. Everything moved in slow motion, almost surreal, as though two worlds collided simultaneously: one of naïve innocence and one of harsh reality.

Amid the chaos, myriad thoughts popped in his head: *Do something!* an inner voice screamed. *Slam your heel on the accelerator until we crash into the parked car ahead of us. That'll create a commotion.*

As if reading his mind, the man grabbed

a clump of his Steve's hair and yanked the drenched mass straight back while applying pressure to the blade, piercing the fleshy tissue on the side of the neck.

The poke drew a trickle of blood and a stifled yelp from Steve staring up at the grey headliner, terrified he was going to die.

"Boy, don't even think about being heroic," the man hissed, his face inches away, their lips almost touching. "There's no way out. Any funny business and you're dead ... like your little friend. Poof! You'll disappear and no one will ever know what happened. Understand?"

"Yessss," Steve gasped, his heart racing like a turbine.

The deranged man released his grip, and said, "To make sure you don't do anything stupid," pulling out chrome-plated handcuffs from under the seat, "I'm going to put these on you, so turn sideways with your hands behind your back."

The hard metal dug into Steve's wrists causing him to wince with each ratcheting notch.

"Now slide down on to the floor and keep your yap buttoned."

Out of options with his arms pinned

from behind like a trussed turkey, Steve slithered down to the floorboard.

In the tight space, he couldn't find a comfortable spot - the hump of the transmission and heater vent restricted him on one side, a pair of lifeless legs trapping him on the other.

The feeling of impending doom roiled through him knowing he was alone to face whatever the monster had in store for him. He wanted to whimper in fear but held back the tears.


CONVINCED THE GUNSHOT went unnoticed, Loren put the car in gear and slowly eased away from the curb.

With an unforeseen calm, relieved the first part of the plan went without a hitch, he turned right at the next residential street. From there he'd make his way to the major thoroughfares leading to the Pasadena Freeway, and ultimately his hideaway.

Mid-way up the debris-strewn road, a mewling groan from the passenger seat pierced the air.

"Ooooooow."

Stunned, Loren slammed on the brakes and the rear end of the Chevy fishtailed across the slick asphalt before coming to a stop in the middle of the block.

He couldn't believe his ears. *Rick-the-prick's not dead? Impossible!*

Chewing feverishly on his bottom lip, he stared at the silhouette leaning against the door - the expendable object in the scheme of things.

Then one of the rabid voices in his head rose to the surface: *Improvise, fucker.*

HE'S STILL ALIVE! Steve's heart thumped as though a syringe of epinephrine had been jabbed in his chest.

From his confined position, legs bent at the knees, he inched his foot forward until it grazed Rick's sneaker and gave it a tap. Within seconds, he received a nudge in return.

*Yes!* he wanted to scream as renewed hope surged through him. The despair rumbling in his gut quickly evaporated, replaced with an urgent sense of purpose - the need to find a way to get them free. *But how?*

The answer came from above with the sound of the driver pounding on the steering column, wailing plaintively in a voice seemingly filled with anguish.

"Oh, shit! What did I do? I made a horrible mistake. Please forgive me Lord."

Befuddled by a combination of chaos and uncertainty, Steve thought the man was speaking to him and jumped at the chance to gain their freedom.

"Mister, take my friend to a hospital," he pleaded. "Just drop us off at the entrance and drive away."

"I can't do that. The doctors will notify the police, and you've seen what I look like and the type of car I'm driving."

Before Steve could respond, the madman blurted out as though he had an epiphany: "I got it! Mother's a nurse and she'll know what to do. We'll go to her house in Pasadena."

Steve's brow creased. *That's almost an hour away.* "Wouldn't it be better to take us to...."

"Shut the fuck up!" the man exploded in a fit of rage. "We'll do things my way, you hear. We're going to see Mother because I'm the one who's in charge. DO-YOU-UNDERSTAND!"

Terrified, Steve cowered and pushed back against the firewall.

In the darkness, Loren silently congratulated himself on delivering an Oscar performance – instilling dread was the quickest way to establish dominance. He could thank Mother for the never-ending lessons. Now he had to convince the *Chosen One* everything would be all right.

To gain the boy's trust, he said, "Sorry for screaming at you. I'm scared because I did something real dumb and took it out on you."

Wedged in the corner of the footwell like a frightened animal, Steve remained silent, fearful of uttering a word.

"You need to stay quiet so I can concentrate how to explain my screw-up to Mother. In the meantime, I have to cover you so you won't know where we're going," Loren said calmly, then he retrieved the Army surplus blankets from the back seat and threw them over his captives.

*I told you*, one of the voices in his head murmured. *Put the fear of God in 'em and you'll get what you want. Now let's haul ass and get home so we can have some fun....*

# CHAPTER 13

**THE HORROR BEGINS**

GATHERING HIS WITS as the car surged ahead, Steve realized less than a couple of minutes had elapsed since the gunshot first rang out - the ensuing bedlam had turned everything into a frenzied blur.

Covered under the coarse wool blanket, warm air blowing in from the heater vent caused him to break out in a sweat. The mixture of salty perspiration and Three Flowers Hair Tonic dribbled down his brow and into his eyes. Helpless to stop the burning, he resorted to blinking repeatedly until the stinging ebbed.

Heading toward the unknown, Steve had no idea how long they had been driving. It could have been minutes. It seemed like hours.

A scene from the Wizard of Oz suddenly popped into in his thoughts; the likeness of a large hourglass with green-faced Margaret Hamilton as the Wicked Witch of the West, cackling with glee while red grains of sand dropped through the narrowed neck of the globe. It sent an icy shiver racing down his back.

The abrupt lurch of the transmission shifting into passing gear snapped him out of his daydream when the Chevy accelerated up what he surmised was a freeway onramp.

Based on the volume of traffic noise, he guessed they were nearing downtown L.A.'s cloverleaf where it veered in multiple directions, providing access to myriad interchanges.

Soon they were traveling along a stretch of gentle s-curves, where the echoed pitch of the tires repeatedly changed from wet pavement to dry pavement, thumping repeatedly as though traversing a series of intermittent tunnels. That's when it dawned on him, they were heading north toward Pasadena on the 101 – the section of Southern California's oldest highway system was unmistakable as it bisected Arroyo Seco Park.

Hypnotized by the drone of the engine, his attention soon drifted and rational thought slipped away, replaced with visions of people pointing fingers, yelling at him: *This is all your fault! You broke curfew for a piece of ass and now look what happened. You got your best friend shot.*

Eventually the car came to an abrupt stop and he awoke foggy headed. *Where the hell are we?*

*WE'RE HOME!* Loren rejoiced to himself after pulling into the driveway of his rental house and coming to a standstill in the backyard.

With the critical element of his objective completed, aside from the minor glitch of not dispatching the boy riding shotgun, everything could go as planned. Rick-the-prick would soon learn the meaning of flipping off the wrong guy.

A corner of his mouth lifted, replaying the harried moments after the gun discharged from the cosmetic case - the confusion running through the Chosen One's head must have been intense. It was paramount to keep him that way. In time, his will to resist would ebb, like taming a wild stallion. All he needed to do was instill unrelenting fear in order to dominate.

*And dominate we will!* shouted one of the rabid alter-egos.

Images of his mother fluttered in Loren's head - from childhood through puberty, she managed to raise him in a constant state of uncertainty, maintaining her dominion over him as he aged. Between the beatings and insatiable lovemaking, he had learned well. *Now it's my turn,* he mused.

FROM UNDER THE covers, Steve inched his

foot forward and tapped Rick's shoe. He got a nudge back. *Good. He's hanging in there.*

From out of nowhere, the blanket was yanked off and he batted his eyes until the vague silhouette of the man sitting behind the wheel came into view.

"Are we at your mother's house?" he asked.

"Yeah. But stay down. I don't want the neighbors snooping so I'm going to pull into the garage. Afterwards, I'll go talk to Mother."

The car idled in place for several agonizing moments without a word spoken.

Then....

THWACK! THWACK!

*What the fuck was that*? Steve wondered. It didn't take long to find out.

THUD! THUD! Two blows smashed the top of his head and stars danced in his eyes.

Suddenly a narrow shaft of light pierced the darkness.

*Flashlight!* Intuitively, Steve feigned unconsciousness and his head lolled to the side.

Like an avalanche, a shocking revelation rumbled through him - the stranger lied, and no one had a clue they had been kidnapped.

A moment later, the beam vanished, and the man got out, closing the door behind him.

With their captor gone, Steve whispered to Rick, "Are you okay?"

"Stomach on fire ... hurts bad."

Not wanting to terrify his buddy, Steve held back they'd been duped. There was no help.

"I don't know what's happening but you got to fake you're unconscious so he won't hit you again. Play possum or something," he said with urgency. "And I'll try to find a way to get us out of this." A faint grinding akin to metal wheels rolling over rough concrete grabbed his attention and he waited until the sound ceased. "You need to..."

The car door opened, and the dome-light flicked on, bathing the interior in a yellowish hue.

Terrified, Steve shut his eyes, then heard the man slide in and engage the transmission.

The car edged forward a few feet,

stopped and backed up, then advanced slowly before coming to a stop again.

Nerve-racking seconds dragged by without a word being uttered.

THWACK! THWACK! THWACK!

Three quick strikes splintered the stillness, and Rick's shoe-tips rattled against Steve's shin.

*Oh God, no!* he thought, bracing himself.

THUD! THUD! The second blow gashed his head and blood flowed down his brow to the tip of his nose and into his mouth. He floated in space momentarily before his head cleared and the blurriness in his eyes faded.

Other than the chirping of crickets, it remained deathly quiet for several agonizing minutes until the car door opened and the interior light flicked on.

Petrified, Steve waited a beat before stealing a quick peek as the man slid out, leaving the door ajar.

In the dim light, all he could see were Rick's legs directly in front of him, his torso skewed to the side, slumped at an unnatural angle.

Knowing he had little time, he whispered, "Talk to me. Are you okay?"

"Noooo," Rick rasped, and he started to whimper.

"Listen, don't cry. And whatever happens, stay awake. Do you understand?" he urged. "Keep tapping me to let me know..." he stopped mid-sentence when he heard the garage door rolling shut, followed by the sound of approaching footsteps. "...Shh, he's coming back."

Once the man got in and closed the door, everything turned black as coal.

Steve tried to penetrate the disorienting gloom and felt as though he'd been sealed inside a crypt.

From above his floorboard perch, a flurry of movement shattered the calm as more blows began to rain down on Rick, the last one sounding like an eggshell cracking.

Holding back the bile burning in his throat, Steve wondered why the rage was directed at Rick and not him? Perhaps he was being spared for a more ominous purpose?

His eyes welled: "Please Lord. Help us," he mouthed as a tear rolled down his cheek. "I'm begging you. Don't let Rick die."

Suddenly, the frenzy ceased, and it became still inside the cabin. The only sound, that of the crazed man wheezing from exertion.

TIME PASSED IN eerie silence, adding to Steve's nightmare. He flashed once more to the image of the *Wicked Witch* and a chill ran down his neck - he sensed time was running out.

Trying to find a more comfortable resting position, he shifted his body and grimaced as a bolt of searing pain shot up his arms. He wanted to scream as the cuffs bit deeply into his wrists, drawing blood.

Unable to tolerate the agony, he steeled himself for another barrage and said, "Mister, can you take the handcuffs off? They're hurting really bad. I promise I won't cause any trouble."

Much to his relief, a voice in the darkness said, "Sure. Move up a little so I can unlock them. Remember no funny business because I don't want to hurt you anymore."

Oddly, Steve felt grateful hearing the words: "... I don't want to hurt you," and did as he was told.

With the shackles removed, he retreated deep into his cubbyhole like a moray eel, his shoulders painfully stiff from having his arms pinned from behind. But it didn't matter. For the moment, he was free.

In the oppressive vacuum, more minutes ticked by without movement, as though time had become inert.

With his back to the firewall, he detected an odd patter from the passenger seat area; slow but steady, like a leaky faucet: *drip ... drip ... drip.*

In need of assurance that his friend was still alive, he reached out to squeeze Rick's ankles. Almost immediately, both legs were whisked away and disappeared into impenetrable abyss.

Steve's heart raced. *Where is he?*

A moment later the sound of cloth being shredded diverted his attention, followed by a cacophony of primitive sounds: slurping, like a dog lapping water, and pitiful mewls amid grunting and muffled squeals.

An unclean stench assaulted his senses and his nostrils flared. *What the hell is he doing?*

After several horrifying minutes, the rocking motion ebbed, and Rick was thrown to his seat like a discarded rag doll.

Steve put his hand on Rick's leg, only to discover it was bare. Shocked, he jerked his hand back as reality blasted to the surface. *I'm next.*

Panicked, as though his heart might burst through his chest, he let lose a stream of pee into his briefs.

A chilling voice interrupted his dread: "Boy, come up here and take off all your things and toss them in the back. You won't be needing them."

Stunned, Steve reeled as cogent thought took flight, confused why he had to strip if the guy was intent on killing him, too.

Without viable options, he maneuvered his way to a spot on the bench seat sandwiched between his dead pal and the driver.

In the tight space, he struggled undressing one layer at a time; first his hefty bomber jacket, then the sweat-soaked shirt.

Unaware his legs had fallen asleep from being crammed on the floorboard, when he tried to lower his jeans, the blood circulated back with a vengeance – the sensation of pins and needles pricked through him like hot spears.

He fought the biting stitch and eased his Levis down until he felt the urine-soaked crotch.

Disgusted with his lack of self-control, he took off his sneakers and socks and tossed everything over his shoulder, and then stared at the cavernous pit beyond the windshield, shivering with fear.

A throaty whisper cut through the bleakness, the tone tinged with a glint of humor: "Uh, you forgot your underwear."

# CHAPTER 14

**LOREN'S PAST REVEALED**

ALARM BELLS PEALED in Steve's head. He couldn't move, couldn't think.

Out of the darkness, a knuckle jabbed the meaty part of his shoulder, hitting a nerve center with precision-like accuracy, sending a stinger racing down his arm.

"I told you to drop your shorts or I'm going to hit you again," he heard the man growl. "Do it now!"

Still recoiling from the painful spasm, Steve reluctantly complied and tossed the soiled briefs over his head and then modestly covered his genitals with his hands.

Sandwiched between his motionless friend and the stranger behind the wheel, he couldn't see either one of them; not their silhouettes, not even his own fingertips trembling atop his lap.

Filled with terror, he steeled himself, waiting for more beatings.

None came.

*Can I fight back?* he wondered. *Even though the guy is twice my size and has a switchblade, I'll die anyway if I don't do anything.*

Breaking his thought, the bench seat suddenly slid back and jerked to an abrupt stop.

Startled, his heart thumped. *What the fuck?*

Out of the black fog—

"Since we have more room, get up on my lap ... facing away from me."

Steve's eyes widened. "Whaddaya mean?" he said, still shaken. "I don't understand."

Without warning, sticky tape sealed his lips and was wrapped around his head several times.

"You talk too much," said the man, grabbing him by the shoulders and lifting him up. "Now slide over here."

*Oh shit!* was Steve's first thought when he felt bare legs and a hardened appendage beneath him.

*How could've I be so stupid? So fucking naïve,* he wanted to scream as reality rose to the surface. Frightened as never before, he would've peed but there was nothing left to drain.

In his rattled state, three things seemed certain: he was trapped in a tomb-like structure, whereabouts unknown; his best friend was dead; and now the crazed monster intended on doing unspeakable things to him, killing him afterward - that's what he had done to Rick; the weird mewling, the heavy panting, the vile stench.

A pair of hands pulled him back to a hairless chest, and then began fondling him.

Steve closed his eyes tightly to block out the indignity now flooding through every cell.

Overcome with shame, cerebral thought ceased to exist - he couldn't concentrate, couldn't move, his brain seemingly off to one side in hibernation mode while the rest of his body functioned on its own.

"There's something I want you to do," the madman whispered in his ear.

Time stood still -


"IN CASE YOU forgot, my name's Loren. And just so you understand, I didn't mean to hurt you but you had to know I was serious," he said, pausing to lick a bead of sweat running down the side of the Steve's neck - the mixture of dripping blood and perspiration arousing him even more.

"Do you realize I waited four years for you? And now you're here. With me! I've never been so happy."

Steve's brow furrowed, not grasping the connection.

"I know your name, but I'd prefer to call you Steven. Is that all right?"

Steve nodded.

"Good. So tell me about yourself. Like how old you are, what grade you're in, the kind of music you listen to. Things like that."

The moment the man began speaking in an affable tone, a part of Steve's thought-process awoke, registering the stark change in demeanor.

"Are you going to kill me, too? he asked meekly."

"Depends on whether you answer my questions and do as you're told."

"Why did you do this to us?"

"If you behave, I'll explain everything later ... in a different place where we'll have lots of time to chat and get better acquainted."

*Later? Different place?* Steve glommed onto the words, interpreting them as a glimmer of hope. Instincts told him if he kept the man busy talking, he wouldn't be thinking about doing other things.

"I'm fifteen," he finally uttered. "The boy you killed ..." his voice wavering as images of his best friend fluttered in his head, "...was only fourteen."

"Wow. I would have bet that you were more like twelve, but it doesn't matter now. Finish what you were saying."

*What a cold-blooded prick*, Steve thought. *No conscience or remorse for what he did. And now the bastard is carrying on as though nothing horrific happened.*

With a deep breath, trying to repress the humiliation of what his body was experiencing, he focused on his dialog with the crazed man.

"Yeah, well, people usually think I'm a lot younger."

Not knowing what to say, he ad-libbed the first thing that came to mind.

"Anyway, I live with my mother and older brother. Both my parents are deaf mutes and I communicate with them in sign language. They got divorced when I turned five and my dad visits me once or twice a month."

Without a stitch of empathy, Loren replied, "It's pretty tough not having a father around while growing up, especially during your formative years. Mine left when I was a kid, too. All because of *Mother*," he said, spitting out the word with disdain. "She's a psychotic nymphomaniac who belongs in a mental institution."

"A psychotic nymphomaniac? What do you mean by that, mister?"

"Please. Call me Loren. Okay?"

"Oh. All right ... Loren," Steve muttered hesitantly, sensing the urgency to keep the monster engaged in conversation.

In the pervasive gloom, a tongue swabbed the back of his neck and he forced himself not to cringe, even though the man's funky breath made his stomach churn.

"Mother's destined for damnation because she's pure evil, a sick mind filled with perversions. But what's really sad is that she's drop-dead gorgeous and could be a double for Natalie Wood."

Gazing at the void beyond the windshield, Steve's eyes flickered at the mention of the famous star - he thought of her as one of the most beautiful women in the world and had seen her movies countless times.

"I can tell you stories about Mother that would make your skin crawl; the depraved things she's done to me and made me do to her. It's almost too bizarre to even talk about," and then his voice faltered.

After a lengthy interlude, as if regaining his composure, he murmured, "She stole my soul. Destroyed it when I was a child."

Loren grasped Steve's hands and placed them atop the steering wheel, and said, "Does your mother give you baths?"

*What the heck?* Steve thought, but kept his mouth in check - his life depended on keeping the man content by treating him as a new-found buddy.

"No. My mom stopped giving me them when I was like five or six."

Driven by the will to survive, he urged the lunatic to continue, unknowingly becoming the interrogator. "Why do you ask?"

Loren went silent for a beat before replying, "You're lucky. For me, the bathtub is where all began."

# CHAPTER 15

**MOTHER**

AT FIRST, GETTING information from Loren had been dicey, like walking a tightrope without a safety net. However, after a bit of innocent coaxing, Steve got him to open up. And open up, he did.

Words spewed from the deranged man while describing his formative years, offering vivid depictions of his family life.

He spoke of parents who fought frequently. Often the arguments escalated into all-out donnybrooks, ending with his mother smashing plates against the wall and his father storming out of the house, disappearing for days on end.

By the time Loren turned eight, the bond with his mother had grown much closer during his father's frequent absences.

"Close in a perverted way...," he whispered, and then his voice trailed off into a long hiatus.

Motionless as a marionette atop a puppeteer's lap, Steve could feel the slow

rise and fall of Loren's chest, waiting
for him to finish his tale.

And he waited.

Anxious to keep the man talking, he
finally broke the silence, and uttered,
"What do you mean perverted way?"

Loren sucked in a deep breath, almost a
shudder.

"It started when my father, Al, left
for good. Without a steady income for
monthly bills, Eleanor, that's *Mother*..." he
said with a tinge of animus, "...asked her
widowed mom to move in and share expenses.

"My nana, Annie, always treated me
lovingly. In fact, she used to call me her
'talented little angel.' Now..." he
snickered, "... she refers to me as her
'handsome lug.'

"Go on," Steve prompted.

"Anyway, she did her best to shield me
when Mother got in one of her violent snits,
but I don't think she ever knew the truth of
her daughter's depravity, and I never told
anyone about the things that were done to
me."

"Really? Like what?"

With a derisive snort, as though being

forced to relive bizarre events, Loren unveiled his family's dirty laundry.

**\*\*\*\***

ALVIN NEESTRUM, known by friends as *Big Al*, migrated from Canada at age twenty-four. Within a week, he secured a decent-paying job at the Helms Bakery on Venice, driving a route in one of their boxy blue and yellow neighborhood vans.

Exceptionally virile, with riveting blue eyes and chiseled features, he was a large man, but thick in the head.

His youthful visions of becoming an actor ended the day he met the woman of his dreams, Eleanor Shanks. Her rare beauty captivated him, and after a few dates, so did her unrelenting sexual appetite. They soon wed and rented an apartment near McArthur Park. One year later she became pregnant.

For nine months Eleanor obsessed over the notion of having a little girl to raise - she even purchased clothes in advance, and spent hours decorating the baby's room with hand-painted pink elephants and giraffes.

But everything changed following a complicated and arduous labor, resulting with her giving birth to a healthy baby boy. Later that same night, the obstetrician at St. Vincent's Hospital informed her she would never be able to conceive again.

The news devastated her. More than anyone imagined.

In the ensuing months following her stay in the hospital, Eleanor's quirky behavior began to surface and grew exponentially over the next two years.

To manage her distress, she found solace dressing Loren in girl's clothes while her husband was at work.

One afternoon Al came home early and discovered his son clad in a lacy yellow outfit with lipstick and makeup on his face.

In a fit of rage, he beat his delusional wife senseless and made her swear to never clothe their child as a girl, or even treat him like one.

After that brutal episode she never dressed up Loren again but would privately refer to him as 'Missy,' or 'Miss Lana Turner', her favorite actress.

Over time, Eleanor's mental state continued to erode, and Al found it increasingly difficult coping with her erratic mood swings and unexpected outbursts. He began drinking heavily and going out with women on the sly.

At one point her condition

deteriorated to such an extent he had her
voluntarily committed to a sanitarium in
Camarillo for six months.

**\*\*\*\***

"THAT'S WHEN HE disappeared forever,"
Loren remarked without a trace of sadness.
"He just up and left. A week later, he
called from Quebec and told Mother to start
divorce proceedings and that she could
retain everything, including child custody."

"Sorry to hear that," Steve
interjected, trying his best to sound
sympathetic.

"While I was growing up," Loren
rambled, "Mother made it her mission in life
to make sure I resented him, constantly
reminding me how he abandoned us for another
woman and brainwashed me into believing all
girls were evil sluts to be shunned."

With hands still draped over the
steering wheel, Steve prompted Loren to
continue, oblivious where he was sitting –
in his mind, his body had ceased to exist,
numbed from the physical abuse. His only
rational thought: Keep the crazed man
talking.

"Tell me about the kind of things your
mother did to you."

"So you want to know more, eh?" Loren

replied, seemingly thankful someone cared about his miserable life.

THE MONOLOGUE BEGAN with him serving up flashbacks of his youth; recalling episodes as a nine-year-old when he and his mother played games in the clawfoot cast iron tub.

They'd frolic in the water, taking their time washing one another. Often, while in a drunken stupor, she would encourage him to explore her body, and whenever he ran his fingers over her nipples or vagina, she would flush and giggle like an innocent schoolgirl being naughty.

Her laughter pleased him, and his puerile mind translated her glee as love for him.

Bath-time rituals were filled with fun and adventure, and in later years, so did the erotic experiences where he became the sole beneficiary of his mother's attention - the one thing he craved more than anything. She made him vow never to reveal what they did; a secret he always cherished.

"Wow!" Steve exclaimed as he took in the sordid details.

Intuitively, he believed his captor needed to liberate years of pent-up emotions, as though he had never spoken a word of his bizarre existence to another soul. Even the man's body language seemed to change while unloading his secretive burden; he appeared comfortable with Steve sitting on his lap as though telling a bedtime story to a toddler.

"You should've told someone, your nana or even a teacher. How come you didn't?"

"I was too young and trusted her. But then as I got older, I came to realize she was a psychotic manipulator who played me like a Stradivarius."

"A Strata-what?"

"A Stradivarius. It's a violin.

"Oh. Must be a new brand because I never heard of one before."

Loren let out a short chuckle.

"Like I was saying..." he went on, his voice abruptly taking on a more serious tone, "...I needed her love, even though she abused me on a regular basis. And with no father-figure at home and seeing Mother crying all the time, I guess I wanted to make her happy. Please her, you know?"

"Damn. You sure had a weird childhood, but I still don't get the bath-sex thing."

"Oh ... yeah," Loren said as if

awakened from a daydream.

"I was about ten, and one night while Annie was out of town, Mother explained why she enjoyed taking baths together. She said it brought back memories of her father when she was a kid."

Whispering, as though unmasking a tale of epic proportions, he said on that particular night she revealed the unnatural relationship she had with her dad, Max.

**★★★★**

THE ROAD TO Eleanor's deviant development began one summer evening when her mother had gone out with a group of friends for a late-night bite to eat. Afterward, they went to a 'Midnight Madness Sale' at the May Co. on Wilshire and Fairfax.

Not wanting to immerse himself into the gaggle of chatty housewives, Max volunteered to stay home and baby sit.

As a sassy eleven-year-old on the cusp of puberty, Eleanor was only too happy to be alone with her handsome father without others vying for his affection.

That night while she watched television, Max seized the opportunity to take a soothing Epsom Salts soak and told her he would leave the bathroom door ajar in

166

case of an emergency.

During a commercial break, she recalled needing to ask him something, so she tiptoed to the room and peeked inside.

Through the steamy mist, she could see him lying back in the tub with his eyes closed, stroking a part of his body she'd never seen before.

Her face flushed when she realized what it was, and a warm tingling fluttered low in her belly while goosebumps raced down her legs.

For some inexplicable reason, watching him masturbate excited her. She didn't understand why. It just did.

Then she did the unthinkable.

Eleanor slid into the room and sidled next to him unnoticed, mesmerized by the erect organ.

When her father opened his eyes and saw her staring at him, he jumped up, barking at her to hand him a towel.

Frozen, gawking at the large appendage jutting at a ninety-degree angle, she paid no heed.

As though in a trance, she reached out

and touched it, and from that moment on she was his....

**** 

"HOLY CRAP," STEVE blurted, interrupting the story. "So, her father did it to her and she followed in his footsteps with you. That is so unreal. Like ... like something I read a couple of years ago."

"Oh? What was it?"

"A friend of mine stole a paperback book from his dad and let me see some of the juicy chapters. I think it was the Tropic of something or other, written by the guy who shacked up with Marilyn Monroe. But I can't remember the name."

From behind he heard a snicker.

"You know Steven, I like you. You're not only pretty bold but perceptive, too. You make me smile."

A slimy tongue slithered across the side of Steve's neck and he winced in disgust.

"You taste yummy. Kind of sweet and salty," Loren murmured, smacking his lips.

"Anyway..." he resumed, "You got the name of the book partly right. It's either the 'Tropic of Cancer' or 'Tropic of

Capricorn', both penned by Henry Miller. The man who married Marilyn Monroe is *Arthur Miller*. And yeah, some of the stuff you read is sort of what we did with each other."

The image of the *Wicked Witch* and the hourglass leaked into Steve's thoughts while Loren carried on like a popinjay, recounting the life-altering event on his twelfth birthday.

His sordid details began with Annie visiting friends in San Francisco for the weekend, and the celebratory evening commenced with Eleanor having her usual three Johnnie Walker's before dinner. This time, however, she offered some to Loren. He recollected how it burned his throat, but the second one went down much smoother and made him feel tipsy.

Once the dishes were put away, they retreated to the bathroom and lit several candles before stripping down and easing into the tub.

Sandwiched between her legs with Loren lying back against her breasts, she wrapped her arms around him and teased him to arousal, then stopped and allowed him to go limp. She repeated the exercise multiple times, thus teaching him the art of self-control.

Afterwards, they got out and padded to the bedroom soaking wet where she made passionate love to him for the first time. Their intimacy lasted several hours and from that night forward, he was hers.

WHILE RELIVING INCESTIOUS exploits, the tempo of Loren's breathing increased, and Steve felt a stiffening grow beneath his legs.

*Damn it!* he cursed himself for being lulled into his captor's fantasy, and quickly sidetracked their conversation.

"So, when are we going to this other place you mentioned?"

There was a long pause.

Suddenly, his body was lifted, and as his head slammed into the headliner, something warm probed his underside.

Throughout the night he had endured beatings and the loss of his companion. Now he faced the ultimate humiliation, knowing he would never be able to live with himself, incapable of expunging the shameful horror.

Worn down by attrition, far beyond the pinnacle of fear, he shook his head: "No. No. No. I won't let you do it!"

In the darkness, the click of the switchblade echoed near his ear.

No longer in control of conscious thought, tears streamed down Steve's face.

"I'd rather be dead than let you do *that* to me," he hissed through clenched teeth while tightening his sphincter muscles. "Go on, kill me because you did it to Rick and you'll do the same to me. So, get it over with!"

The tip of the blade scratched his cheek.

"Are you ready to die?" said Loren. "Just because I want you. All I ever needed was a boy like you to love me. We'd be so happy together. You'll see. It'll only be for a year, then I'll set you free."

"I'll never be the way you want me to be. Never!"

"Well, since you don't want to cooperate, maybe I'll lop off your nuts and save your cock for dessert. How does that sound?"

Chest heaving, Steve spiraled deeper into the abyss of hopelessness.

From the passenger side of the car, a pitiful moan interrupted the madness....

# CHAPTER 16

**BIZARRE TWIST**

ANOTHER SURGE OF adrenaline steamrolled through Steve the moment he heard the sound.

"Rick," he gasped. "He's alive!"

His elation was short-lived.

"Get the fuck off me," Loren growled, pushing him to the floor like an unwanted toy.

From the seat above.

THWACK! THWACK! THWACK!

"This'll teach you to flip me off, you little prick. Some people don't take kindly to being disrespected..."

THWACK! THWACK! THWACK!

"...especially if they have a mean streak in 'em like me," Loren grunted while pummeling Rick.

In the cramped confines, Steve's face screwed into a grimace and pulled his knees to his chest as a wave of guilt crashed through him - relieved he wasn't the one being beaten.

*What the hell do I need to do to get rid of this useless cocksucker?* Loren wondered as he hammered away.

From deep within, a virulent alter-ego bellowed: *Wake up, dummy! He's been shot and the bullet fragmented somewhere inside of him. Now are you going to let him stand our way? Hit him harder!*

THWACK! THWACK!

Another voice broke in: *Stop being so anxious getting your rocks off. We've got plenty of time for that. Remember the objective?*

Exhausted, his head full of static, Loren needed to restrain the beasts - they only added to his confusion. Time to take a break and regroup.


THE SAVAGE BEATING stopped, and a tense stillness once again filled the air.

Steve strained to detect movement from above, trying to think of a way to keep the madman away from Rick.

The seconds oozed by and the terrifying nightmare continued to soak up all the moisture in his mouth - his throat was so parched it pained him to swallow. Even his tongue had the texture of sun-dried leather.

"Is there any water?" he finally rasped, piercing the griping stillness.

The question went unanswered.

Then a crazy notion popped into Steve's head: "You still want to be friends, don't you?" Coiled tight as a watch spring, he waited, hoping to re-connect.

The welcoming words from the Chosen One snagged Loren from the cacophony assaulting his senses. *He's speaking to me. He must want me!*

"Yes!" he replied anxiously, desperate to re-establish their bond. He needed time to convince the boy they belonged together – at least until he carried out the final chapter of his plan.

"There's water out back. Stay where you are and I'll bring some. Promise not to do anything dumb."

"I won't."

After a brief pause, Loren got out and vanished into the void.

With the creak of the trunk opening, Steve whispered to Rick. "Can you hear me? Your possum trick saved my life. Thanks."

"Head throbbing ... stomach on fire."

"Sorry you're hurting. I'm still trying to get us out of this. Don't make any more noise because he hates your interruptions when he's talking to me. Hang in the best you can, and I'll keep him from..."

The approaching footsteps caught his attention. "Shh! He's coming back."

The door opened wide and the interior light illuminated the cabin.

For a fleeting moment before Loren slid into the car, Steve observed streaks of blood smeared over the man's bare thighs. The sight sickened him, and anger began to percolate in his gut.

Once the door closed and again bathed in darkness, the familiar baritone voice of his captor beckoned him up to the seat.

Sandwiched uncomfortably between two naked bodies, a large plastic container was thrust against Steve's chest. Startled, he found the neck, and after sniffing the contents, greedily chugged the cool water.

He smacked his lips after his thirst was quenched and said, "Can I give some to my friend?"

"I don't want to waste any on him."

"Please?"

"Okay, but only a little. He doesn't need much."

Like a blind person in an unfamiliar room, Steve groped for Rick's face, fumbling until he found his mouth. He let him take a sip, and after hearing him gulp twice, eased the jug away.

Just as he was about to take another swig for himself, a pair of hands materialized out of thin air and yanked the bottle from him, leaving behind a trail of drops dribbling down his chin.

"Lean forward. I've got to put something over your buddy's big yap so we won't be disturbed again."

Heeding the unsettling words, Steve reached for the dashboard and rested his cheek against the glossy metal surface, all the while listening to the rustling from behind.

*The man needs to talk!* his sixth sense screamed, realizing he had somehow emerged as the newfound confidant of a bloodthirsty psychopath. *Just do what he wants and you might make it out of this alive.*

"C'mere Steven. Hop back up on my lap."

PERCHED ATOP SWEATY thighs, Steve took in a deep breath and steeled himself as hands began to fondle him again - his face flushed with shame while his body continued to betray him.

"This reminds me of when I was thirteen," Loren murmured. "There was this eight-year-old I babysat. Whenever his mother went out for a night on the town, he and I would strip down and get in the bathtub and then we'd wash each other, and I'd fiddle with him the same way I'm touching you now.

In the dark, Loren let out a snicker.

"The kid didn't understand what to do at first. For him it was all naive fun and new experiences, like the ones I used to have with Mother. But after several months of babysitting him, the boy became obsessed with me and would do anything I asked; just as you will."

The thought of being the crazed man's sex toy horrified Steve, and he quickly changed the topic: "So you were a teenager when you realized you were queer?"

"What the hell are you talking about?" Loren shot back angrily. "I'm not a flaming fag! Do I look like one, or talk like one?"

"No."

"You're damned right. Do you know the meaning of the term, 'Pedophile'?"

"Uh-uh."

"It comes from the Greek word: Paidophilos. In essence, it's an adult who likes children -- sexually. Ever since my first experience with my neighbor, I found that I'm attracted to boys on the brink of puberty. You know, eleven and twelve-year-olds. For some reason they turn me on," he cooed while nibbling on Steve's earlobe.

"I wasn't able to find a suitable replacement until now, even though you're not as young as I would've liked."

"Where is he?" Steve asked, wondering if the monster kidnapped him, too - his mind racing in circles recalling the scene after the gunshot first rang out: *'...I killed before and won't hesitate to do it again.'*

"His name was Johnny..." said Loren, and quickly corrected himself, "...Is Johnny. The family moved from the old neighborhood quite a while ago, and I dreamt about him a lot while jerking off under the covers. Eventually those dreams faded."

"Does anyone else know about...?"

"Only you."

"And Johnny. Right?"

"I'm not worried about him anymore."

Steve's brow arched. *Did he kill him?*

"What about your mom?" he pressed.

"Hah! If she found out, she'd go off the deep-end and castrate me while I was sleeping. She even said as much."

"A big guy like you, afraid of his mother?"

"Kind of. I grew up terrified of her because she used to haul off and whip me with a belt for no reason; mostly when she forgot her medications. The only time I ever felt secure with her was when we were in the tub or in bed having sex."

Loren went silent for a moment, as though recalling a series of memorable events in his life.

"As time passed," he continued, "our escapades got stale. To tell the truth, I preferred being with my little pal a hell of a lot more because *I* was the teacher."

A hardening beneath Steve's legs alarmed him and he hastily shifted the subject.

"Do you hate her for what she's done to you?"

The question took Loren by surprise.

"Yeah. I do," he finally replied, his head bobbing in the dark. Then, "No! Of course I don't. She's Mother!"

Another long pause.

"Well, fucking-A! I don't know," he blurted, sounding rattled. "Sometimes a part of me despises her so much I want to wrap my hands around her beautiful neck...," then his voice trailed off into a whisper of resignation, "...but I usually give in to her demands like I was taught."

While searching for appropriate things to say, the left side of Steve's head began to throb fiercely, and his thoughts scattered in countless directions.

"Life's been confusing for me since I was a child," Loren elaborated. "Do you know that I've never fooled around with another woman? To mess with one would be like cheating on Mother."

"Did you ever have feelings for a girl when you were growing up?"

"Good looking as I am, they scare the hell out of me. I know they want me, always flashing me with hungry eyes, ready to jump in the sack at the drop of a dime. Mother warned me to keep away from them because they're immoral and wicked and would never

180

love me the way she did. At least that was what she drummed into me."

"Uh huh," Steve uttered, feigning interest.

"An hour before I left her apartment tonight, I fucked her brains out until she begged me to stop," Loren bragged. "Funny thing though, she doesn't turn me on anymore and I had to fake my third orgasm.

"Really?"

"Yeah. I try to accommodate her needs, but it ain't the same as it was with Johnny, or even now with you sitting here on my lap talking like friends. Do you understand?"

Steve nodded, and then blinked several times, forcing himself to stay alert - he'd run out of things to talk about. Yet, there was something gnawing at him, a button to push that might set them free. The inkling buzzed in his head like a pesky fly.

Then it struck him.

"Why do you call her, MOTHER? Not once have you referred to her as, *Mom*."

Silence.

"Seems as though the only time she shows you affection is when she's insecure or horny, something a typical mother would never dream of doing to her son."

"Hmph. You're pretty perceptive. Bet you do well at school."

Steve didn't - he flashed back to a memo one of his teachers wrote to his parents: '...*although his test scores are borderline average, possibly due to laziness, your son's a lot wiser than his years and extremely intuitive.*'

"I think you may be right about Mother ... uh ... I mean, *Mom*," Loren stammered as if uttering the word for the first time in his life.

"Do you play a musical instrument?" he asked out of the blue.

*What the hell? He's all over the place. Where's he going with this?* Steve wondered; thankful the man couldn't see the expression on his face.

"Not recently," he replied calmly. "I played the clarinet in junior high but gave up when I graduated. What about you?"

"My passion is the piano. Not to toot my own horn but I'm damn good. My instructors called me a prodigy."

"You're kidding?"

"Nope. In fact, one of my coaches told

me if I put forth some effort, I could be one of the youngest members to join the Philharmonic."

"Wow."

"See, when I'm on the bench tickling the ivories, it makes all the sounds in my head disappear."

Not grasping the link, Steve sloughed it off as more nonsensical gibberish from a lunatic.

With his captor relaxed, seemingly satisfied chatting like two old pals, he thought the time might be right to let his instincts guide him.

"I need to say something and hope you won't be pissed off for asking."

"I'm not planning on hurting you. You're much too valuable to me. More than you can imagine."

"Alright. Why did you do this to us when you could be someone special?"

"I've thought about it but can't seem to contain myself at times. And it's getting worse. These inner voices keep telling me what to do. There's moments when things are crystal clear, then everything becomes foggy and I go off, as if I'm no longer in control of my mind."

"Like your mother," Steve said.

"Hmm. When I was eighteen, I lived on my own for several months and spent time at the library researching schizophrenia. It's hereditary, they say."

"I didn't know that."

"Yeah. I'm ten times more likely to have it than other people. That means I could wind up being crazy just like Mother ... um, I mean ... my mom," his voice softening as though he now appreciated the sound of the word.

Steve's first thought: he wouldn't have to wait, he's already deranged, but his sixth sense cautioned him to tread cautiously while feeding the monster's twisted psyche.

"Listen, based on what you've told me about your life, I think you're probably a good person who was brainwashed by someone totally screwed up," he said, giving careful thought what to say next.

"You could be an accomplished musician if you really wanted, but you're always mixed up. Right?"

Steve felt a nod from behind.

Knowing the next few words out of his mouth were critical, he drew in a breath and

184

said, "I've got an idea that will solve all your problems."

"Go on."

"I'm your friend ... and I think you need outside help. Like in an institution where you'll be cared for, and your mother and Annie will understand what you did and why."

Once the words left his lips, he prayed there wouldn't be any radical shift in body language. Sensing none, he talked for his life.

"I want you to get well. But first we need to get my buddy to a hospital. After that, you can turn yourself in and I'll help in any way I can."

"Institutionalized... safe haven ... forgiveness. Hmmm?" Loren mumbled, contemplating new strategies amidst the turmoil in his head.

Before Steve could press the issue, pitiful groans from the other side of the car interrupted them. *Oh shit, not now.*

He heard Loren mutter under his breath, "What the fuck..." before he was shoved against the steering column.

A beefy shoulder kept him in place, and from behind he heard a gagging noise as though someone were being choked.

In an instant, Steve knew what was happening. Panicked, pushed his back into Loren's chest and locked his arms against the steering wheel for leverage.

The overhead light suddenly flicked on and a meaty paw grabbed the top of his blood-caked pompadour, yanking it sideways.

As his head swiveled like a bobble-head doll, he caught a flash of Rick, frozen in time - duct tape stretched across a bloodied face, eyes filled with terror.

With a feral snarl, Loren hissed, "Steven, you betrayed me, you sonofabitch!"

The light abruptly disappeared, and in the darkness, fingernails began to claw feverishly at Steve's hands tightly wrapped around the steering wheel, digging into them with unbridled fury.

Overpowered by the enraged man, he held fast until his grip gave way and was forcibly shoved down to the floor.

Horror darting through every cell, he curled into a fetal position believing Loren had finally snapped and time had just run out for his best friend.

Swoosh ... THWACK! Swoosh ... THWACK!

The car rocked as Loren's arm worked like a piston, raining blows down on Rick. Steve lost count - perhaps fifteen or twenty.

He tried to block out the sickening sound while fragments pelted his face and blood spurted over his body.

"Stop it! Stop it!" he finally cried out, unable to tolerate the madness. "You're killing him! Please, I'm begging you. Let him live and I'll do whatever you want, be whatever you want," he sobbed as tears streamed down his face and strings of snot oozed from his nose.

WHAM! WHAM! Two quick strikes cracked the side of his head. Dazed, he mouthed the word, "Rick...," before spiraling downward into a vast black hole.

*WHAT THE HELL are you doing?* screeched one of Loren's alter-egos. *You're screwing up everything! The boy thinks you're some kind of hideous fiend. He didn't betray you. He said he was trying to help. You don't want to be like Mother. Or do you?*

Another voice chimed in, livid and fomenting with rage: *To hell with her for crissake! The cunt destroyed your life. You should've strangled the bitch when you had the chance.*

A third voice jumped into the fray: *Steven's right! He wants to be your friend. You must see that by now.*

*You pathetic pussy!* the one frenzied beast persisted. *Finish what you started so you can drag him in the house and show him who's the boss. Think of the pleasure – how he'll taste.*

*Look what you've done,* said the first inner voice. *Don't hurt him anymore. You can't ... you mustn't!*

Loren's eyes welled as he rambled, "Slow down. Need to think. Re-calculate. Improvise. Adapt. The Becoming of One."

Lapsing in and out of consciousness, Steve barely overheard the jabbering from above.

The mumbling finally subsided, and several terrifying minutes drifted by in silence.

From the impenetrable blackness, Loren suddenly wailed, "I give up!" "I can't do this anymore."

*Nooooooooo!* the malevolent voice shrieked. *Don't pay attention to the others. They'll only confuse you. I can get us through---*

*Shut up! All of you.* Loren barked to

the dissonance in his head - throughout the night he let them interfere instead of using them; he didn't want their constant bickering, always at war with each another. *I've got it all figured out and don't need your advice for now.*

With his face buried in his hands, he said aloud, "I don't deserve to live. I just want to die."

Still woozy, the words rapidly cleared through the fog in Steve's head.

"Did you say ... you want to die?"

"Yes."

"Why don't you ... um ... commit suicide?"

"I'm too chickenshit to do it myself," Loren snuffled. "I just wish someone would put me out of my misery."

Without forethought, as though the miracle might somehow evaporate into thin air, Steve said, "If that's what you want ... I'll do it."

# CHAPTER 17

**THE MYSTERY UNRAVELS**

"YOU'D DO THAT for me?" Loren said, wiping his nose with the back of his hand.

Scrunched on the floorboard with his heart thumping like a kettledrum, Steve drew in a breath and said casually, "Well, yeah, but only if you want me to."

A pair of hands materialized out of the black velvet and grabbed him by the shoulders. He flinched, frightened of being walloped again.

"Don't worry," Loren cooed, gently tugging him up to the seat. "I promise I'm not going to hurt you anymore. It's over."

Motionless as a statue, Steve stared at the gaping pit beyond the windshield while convoluted notions zipped through his head. *Is it really over?*

A wave of clarity suddenly cascaded into his thoughts, reminding him to not allow the desire for retribution cloud his thinking, something inculcated from his brother; words and inflection had to be measured knowing the ticking time-bomb next to him could explode at any moment. He prayed Rick wouldn't make any noise.

"You despise me for what I've done," Loren sighed deceitfully, interrupting the lull, all the while checking off adjustments to his revised plan - he wanted to trifle with the lad.

*I can't believe you're that fucking devious*, roared a voice in his head. *Like killing two birds with one stone, eh?*

An evil smirk tightened Loren's lips.

Warily, Steve said, "No, I don't hate you. I know what you must be going through and I want to help." Hesitantly, almost as an afterthought, he added, "How do you want me to do it?"

"With my .22."

Steve's heart raced.

"If I hand you the gun, give me your word you'll use it to kill me."

"Well, okay ... but only because that's what *you* want."


AFTER LOREN GOT out of the car, Steve wasted no time following, skimming his bare ass across the perspiration-soaked seat.

When he stood upright, both knees buckled so he rested an arm on the side-panel for support while bouncing up and down on his toes to stretch his cramped calves.

The shaft of light from the interior illuminated the ground around his blood-covered feet, and as he shuffled about, his footprints left dark smudges on the cold concrete.

Once Loren disappeared into the black void, Steve ducked back inside and scooted close to Rick slumped against the door-panel.

"It's me," he said softly, stealing a nervous peek at the rear window. "If you're alive, don't talk, just nod."

There was no response. No movement. Not even a quiver. He prodded harder, nudging a shoulder.

An eye suddenly popped open, staring up at the headliner like a dead fish. It blinked once; then again, only faster.

Relieved, Steve patted Rick's arm. "Hang on, buddy. We're almost home-free," he said before easing himself out the door and making his way toward the faint glow at the back of the car.

The opened trunk provided just enough light for Steve to take in Loren's blood-streaked torso.

Repulsed, he turned away and said, "I'd like to put on my clothes ... if you don't mind."

"Oh yeah. Go ahead. And while you're at it, bring my things, too."


*WHERE'S THE FREAKING gun?* Steve wondered, as he rummaged through the pile of clothing on the back seat. *The sonofabitch must've hidden it someplace else.*

On the threshold of freedom, he quickly snagged his pants, paying little attention finding his soiled skivvies, shirt, or shoes.

Crumpled on the floor, he spotted Rick's jeans as he backed off and tossed them up front so he could help him dress later.

After edging out and quietly closing the door, Steve made his way to Loren and handed him his clothes, then modestly turned and slipped into his Levis, all the while making note of his surroundings.

In the pervasive gloom, the musty-smelling structure resembled a cavernous vault without boundaries, he thought, sending goose bumps racing down his arms.

Unnerved, he averted the eerie unknown and peered into the cluttered trunk while Loren was getting dressed.

The first thing that caught his attention was a white child-size tee-shirt splattered with stains resembling dried blood.

Inquisitively, he lifted it up for a closer look only to discover a wood-handled saw concealed underneath.

He recognized the tool at once and thought of his childhood and the frequent visits to Stein's Kosher Butcher Shop with his Ashkenazi grandmother – he recalled watching the elderly store owner adorned with a yarmulke, making prayers while cutting through the hanging half-torso of a skinned cow as easily as if slicing a loaf of bread.

The hair on the back of Steve's neck bristled and he took a step back - his instincts screamed the cleaver had a more ominous function, intensifying his resolve to get his hands on the gun.

"Can I take the handcuffs off my buddy," he said.

Annoyed, Loren grumbled, "If you must," fishing a small key from his pocket. "Now hurry up. We don't have all day."

The far side of the car was even spookier, so Steve took extra care slowly padding his way to the passenger side, apprehensive another monster might leap out of the darkness and whack him with a machete.

Cautiously, he eased the door open and gingerly propped Rick upright with one hand while unlocking the cuffs with the other, chucking them to the floorboard.

Pressed for time, he made the dreadful mistake of glancing at Rick's head – portions of scalp were flayed to the bone, his face layered with blood, some bubbling through tape wrapped around his mouth.

Sickened by the gore, Steve spun away and threw up a stream of yellow bile, then wiped the goo from his chin with a forearm and stuck his head back inside.

"Couldn't find your drawers," he whispered, "so I'm going to slide your pants on you as best I can."

He reached for the switchblade on the dash and cut away the sticky wrapping.

"Is that better?"

"Dizzy ... head pounding," Rick rasped in labored breaths. "Stomach hurts ... bad," pointing to a spot low on his belly.

Steve noticed the half-inch polyp-like protrusion and assumed it might've been a bullet fragment trapped beneath layers of skin.

Fighting time, he haphazardly crammed Rick's legs into the Levis.

"Owww!" No more..." Rick whimpered.

"Sorry. I'll take it easy," Steve said, wrestling with the heavy denim fabric, carefully inching it up each leg.

Once he got the jeans on, purposely leaving the fly unbuttoned, his voice turned icy: "I'll be right back. I'm going to kill the motherfucker before I call the cops."


AT THE SOUND of the Chosen One approaching, Loren hastily lowered the lid.

"Steven, you startled me. I didn't hear you coming," he said, quickly leading him away by the arm. "Let me show you my creation."

The dome-light flickered back to life when the driver-side door opened, bathing the left side of Rick's half-naked body in a yellowish hue with his head obscured in the shadows.

*Good. He's playing possum*, Steve thought.

Pulling the backrest forward, Loren pointed to a nondescript vinyl travel case atop the back seat.

To get a better view, Steve leaned in and eyeballed a length of cable extending from one end of the container, observing its path snaking to the driver's side where it connected to a bicycle handbrake lever affixed to a section of plumber's pipe.

His brow furrowed. *What the hell?*

Puzzled, he glanced over his shoulder at his tormentor standing behind him, beaming.

"Ta-da! It's my remote control. Pretty clever, huh?" Loren boasted. "Here, let me show you how it works." Like an eager child, he reached in and unlatched the box.

Steve's jaw clenched when he spotted the upside-down steel-blue revolver. It was fastened in place by aluminum strapping with a jerry-rigged brake caliper encompassing the trigger-guard, along with several white hand towels stuffed inside the case.

*Probably to muffle the sound*, he thought, amazed at the crude simplicity of the device. *Looks like something Alfred Hitchcock might've dreamed up.*

With screwdriver in hand, Loren freed

the firearm and held it out for inspection.

"Have you ever fired one before?"

"Don't know much about them," Steve said.

"No problem, I'll show you," Loren replied, aiming the barrel down at the ground, then flipping the cylinder open to reveal a single spent brass casing.

"This is a nine-shot .22. Now that it's empty, I'm going to re-load it," then he turned without a word and walked away, disappearing into the blanket of black fog.

As Steve was about to follow, the shimmer from an object partially tucked under the seat caught his eye. Curious, he reached down and retrieved a pair of heavy-duty vise-grips.

Weighty in his hand, he raised it to the dome light - clumps of hair and bits of bloodied flesh were wedged between the jagged teeth.

Anger swelled his chest and his nostrils flared, realizing that was what they had been beaten with. *No wonder Rick's head is all fucked up.*

Returning the hefty wrench to where he found it, he thought to himself, *the bastard is going to die, except it'll be a lot slower and far more painful....*

# CHAPTER 18

## RIDE TO FREEDOM

LOREN REMOVED THE spent casing and snapped the empty cylinder back in place.

Out of the corner of his eye he caught sight of the Chosen One examining the vise-grips. His mouth tightened, knowing what must be going through the kid's head.

*Steven wants revenge*, whispered an inner voice. *Good.*

Loren put the pistol down and grabbed a clean hand towel wedged next to the spare tire. With water from the Tupperware jug, he dowsed the cloth and wiped the taped gun grip thoroughly, then proceeded to wash the blood from his face, arms and chest. After drying himself, he donned his denim jacket and put a single .22 round in his pocket.

At the sound of the boy approaching, he used the same dampened rag to grasp the barrel-end of the revolver and held it out.

Steve reached for it - a bit too eagerly.

A foot taller than the Chosen One,

Loren's eyes went flinty, and he dangled the weapon high in the air as though offering a treat to a begging dog.

"You want to get your hands on this, don't you?"

*Ding! Ding!* The alarm bells pealed in Steve's head. *I'm being played.*

"Not really," he retorted with indifference, trying to recapture some of his cockiness, hoping his thumping heart wouldn't betray him.

The evil smirk on Loren's face slowly faded, and he handed Steve the gun, butt-first.

"All you've got to do is cock the hammer and squeeze the trigger repeatedly," he said, using the side of his finger to guide the muzzle to his chest. "Understand?"

"Yep. Just aim it at your heart and pull the trigger nine times."


AT FIRST THE duct-taped grip seemed awkward in his hand yet comforting as though it were a talisman. Steve wondered if the feeling stemmed from the control he now possessed or simply relief the reign of terror might soon be over. Whatever the case, he had the loaded gun and that's all that mattered.

"Time to live up to your word."

Steve's mind whirled — too many convoluted thoughts spinning in his head.

"Where are we?" he asked.

"In a garage. At my house."

"No, I mean what street? What city?"

Loren chuckled, enjoying the taunting moment. "We're on Fair Oaks in Pasadena. Why?"

"You need to call for an ambulance."

"Uh ... I don't have a telephone."

"Oh?" Steve said, lifting a skeptical eyebrow, his cluttered mind trying to check off options.

"Well, what time is it now?"

"A little after four in the morning."

*Only four? Seems like fucking forever*, Steve thought.

Searching his memory, he recalled Fair Oaks as a north-south artery but couldn't remember if the main drag connected to the freeway.

The stubborn migraine-strength headache

hammering away at the left side of his head flared and the throbbing fragmented his thinking even more.

His priority: get help for Rick. All that came to mind was the 24-hour emergency facility at the Children's Hospital on the eastern fringe of Hollywood – that's where his mother would take him every time he got sick or had a careless accident.

The image of a large shopping plaza a block away flashed in his head. *At this hour, especially on a Sunday, the place will be empty. Perfect*, he thought.

Never taught how to drive, he said, "Since you don't have a phone, I can't shoot you until you take us to a hospital, or someplace close to one."

"Whaaat? No fucking way!" Loren exclaimed angrily, taking a menacing step forward. "You told me you'd do it, so what's the hang-up?"

"Look, I said I'll do it and I will," Steve replied, standing his ground.

"Do you know where the Children's Hospital is on Sunset off Vermont? There's a big retail center down the street from the ER and it'll be deserted this time of the morning. Whether I kill you here or in the parking lot shouldn't make any difference," he said with an air of finality.

"Yeah, I know where you're talking about," Loren said, recalculating and adjusting on the fly — Eleanor's apartment was less than a mile away and he knew the open-air shopping plaza well, visualizing the clustered mall with secluded recesses between the storefronts.

*This is going to be so much fun*, an inner voice said.

"All right ... but remember your promise. Besides, just because you're holding a gun, it don't mean diddly-squat. Now put a lid on the excuses and climb in the car."

Steve's heart raced - they were almost free but was unsettled by the furtive remark, '...it don't mean diddly-squat'. *What did he mean by that?*

Sliding across the seat, he heard the faint squeal of hinges followed by the grating of door wheels from deep inside the black pit.

He leaned over to Rick, and whispered, "We're going to get you help. Keep quiet and everything'll be okay."

The response was a pitiful moan.

In the dim light, Steve looked down at the revolver in his hand and his thumb brushed the hammer - for the first time

since their ordeal began, he felt marginally
secure.

A few seconds later Loren got in and
started the engine, then flipped on the
headlamps and shifted the transmission into
reverse.

The Chevy slowly edged out of the
gloomy structure, affording Steve the
opportunity to survey the interior.

The bright beams illuminated the oil-
stained concrete and the tar-paper sheathing
covering the walls; off to the side, sacks
of cement were stacked on top of each other
with rolls of chicken wire propped against
them, and in one of the corners, he spotted
military duffel bags atop an old push-mower.
Otherwise, the musty wooden edifice appeared
to be without the usual clutter; no crowded
shelves, no dusty cardboard boxes, not even
a workbench or pegboard loaded with tools.

He thought it odd but dismissed the
observation - they were headed to freedom.

As they backed into the open, Steve
noticed a short flight of stairs with
wrought-iron side railings leading to the
rear of a weathered clapboard house.

The car crept along a narrow driveway
with a mowed strip of grass down the middle,
and as they passed by the front porch, Steve
glanced at the vertical row of black

numerals affixed to an ornate support pilar: *2014*.

For some inexplicable reason, he silently repeated the number several times, and let out a sigh when they turned onto the street, relieved to be on the road away from the vault of horrors.


THE PASSING STORM from the evening left the streets laden with puddles while remnants of angry clouds still hung overhead, capable of erupting at any moment.

"If it doesn't rain, it should take about half an hour to get Vermont." Then Loren paused a beat, and said, "Are you nervous about killing me?"

"Well yeah," Steve lied. "It's not every day somebody asks you to be their executioner. You sure you want to do this?"

There was no response.

The silence troubled him, much like the unease when he first entered the car at the Chevron station. His intuition had warned him then, but he paid little heed.

Exhausted from being at death's door, the flow of adrenaline continued to ebb, yet the side of his head pounded with a greater ferocity and kept him vigilant.

To take his mind off the unrelenting throbbing, he eyed the darkened houses lining the street as they cruised south on Fair Oaks Boulevard, and thought about the people living in them, sleeping safely in warm beds.

Did they have any idea a blood-thirsty psychopath lived in the same neighborhood, perhaps stalking their children? *Not a snowball's chance in hell*, he thought.


AFTER ENTERING THE 101 toward downtown L.A., the quivering in Steve's gut festered while gazing at the white lane markers dotting the four-lane highway.

Nestled between Rick and the fiend who destroyed their lives, he was overwhelmed with conflicted emotions: reserved euphoria to be heading for safety; masked anxiety for the upcoming task.

On one hand, he believed the monster deserved to be put to death; in the worst possible way. But the words, '*Thou shalt not kill*' kept creeping into his head. Religious tenets declared taking a life a mortal sin ... *unless it was in self-defense*, he quickly rationalized.

*Was the man still a threat?* The more he pondered, the answer rose to the surface with a renewed clarity: he was a danger to everyone; a cold-blooded killer, willing to hurt innocent people without a lick of remorse.

The desire for retribution once again dribbled through him - he was tired of dancing with the devil and needed to put an end to it.

'*Thou shalt not...*' *Shut the fuck up*! he screamed to nagging inner voice. There had to be a price to pay for the unspeakable things that would forever be seared into his memory.

*The sonofabitch is going to die,* he affirmed, *but he needs to suffer.*

A childish notion pecked into his thoughts: *What if I put a bullet in the bastards kneecap, disabling him. Then while he squirmed in agony, lay the barrel against that repulsive appendage and blast several rounds into him. Make him wail like a newborn and give him a taste of his own medicine.*

A corner of his mouth twitched as the scene played out.

★★★★

DEEP WITHIN THE bowels of hell, Rick continued to lapse in and out of consciousness as though he'd been thrust into a blazing inferno, enduring gut-wrenching spasms and penetrating hot flashes. He wanted to scream but his lips were tightly sealed.

A piercing sensation pushed through the chimera like an ice pick, stirring him awake.

Groggy, he sensed he was in a moving vehicle with someone seated next to him. He cast a blurry glance to his left: *It's Steve and he's holding a gun! No way*, he thought while tiny black filaments continued to float across his eyes.

In the never-ending fog, the beating of his heart slowed, thumping softly in his chest. Soon, his vision tunneled down and peripheral sounds grew more distant, becoming fainter and fainter.

Then, like India ink spilled on a blotter, shadows encroached until his eyes closed and his world of pain ceased to exist....

# CHAPTER 19

**RETRIBUTION**

TRAFFIC ON THE 101 was sparse at four in the morning as they cut south towards Children's Hospital.

Every few minutes a paneled delivery truck or bulky semi traveling to parts unknown would whisk by with brake lights flashing while they traversed the series of s-curves.

Steve recalled tracking the same route when they entered the long tunnels bisecting Arroyo Seco Park, only then, they were heading north, with him handcuffed from behind crammed against the floorboard and Rick softly moaning from the seat above.

Off in the distance, he gazed at the clouds to the west breaking up, forming small grayish-white fluffy pillows floating over the onyx sky. They look so innocent, he thought, a stark reminder of his carefree existence twenty-four hours earlier.

He looked away and stole a peek at the speedometer: *Hells bells, we're only doing sixty!* "Can't you go any faster?"

"Don't want to be stopped by the cops, you know. Remember, you're supposed to kill me."

Steve stared at him for a long moment and nodded.

Before long, the downtown cloverleaf loomed ahead, and they veered toward the Hollywood Freeway interchange. Minutes later they rolled to a stop at the end of the Vermont off-ramp.

Before making a right turn, Loren shot a glance through the blood-streaked passenger window and thought of his mother and Annie sleeping at home blocks away, unaware of the atrocities he committed. Unsettled, he gnawed feverishly on his bottom lip, and then goosed the gas pedal when the light turned green.


WAVES OF UNCERTAINTY washed through Steve's veins like a babbling brook; soon he would be forced to take a person's life, much like a hardened executioner fulfilling their task.

Anxiety continued to mount, and the hand holding the revolver trembled slightly as a bead of sweat trickled down the side of his neck.

Where was the overwhelming desire for retribution, he wondered, desperately needing to stoke the feeling once again.

...*Mind games*, he told himself, as
though playing high-speed chess, with moves
and countermoves zipping through his head.

He knew his captor was a diabolical
man, cunning enough to create the illusion
of remorse - he'd witnessed the out-of-
control rage and abrupt apologetic mood
swings throughout the night. Although they
had talked for hours, he suspected there was
something more sinister about the man, far
more craven than he could fathom.

His hackles rose visualizing the images
of being violated and the horrible sounds of
Rick being savagely beaten in the oppressive
darkness. Steve's stomach roiled in its
juices while the unforgettable nightmare
filtered through his memory.

'*Get revenge*' most people would say -
especially Howard. On the other hand, Shel
would have said, '*If you've got a rabid dog,
put 'em down quick and move on with your
life.*'

Inane ideas kept pecking away, making
it difficult to think clearly. Instincts had
helped him navigate through the reign of
terror - but that was before he had the gun.
Now, the notion of intentionally taking
someone's life took on a whole new meaning.

Initially, the .22 clutched in his hand

had provided him with a sense of protective bravado, but now he wasn't sure if the security was real or part of a grand scheme. *With my bloody fingerprints all over the damn thing!*

*...More mind games.* He closed his eyes briefly, recalling the pistol being handed to him by the barrel-end. At the time he hadn't given it much thought – freedom was all that mattered. *Did Loren wipe his own prints off the grip before handing it over? Why? And for what purpose?*


APPROACHING SUNSET BOULEVARD, Steve spotted the unlit plaza on the corner off to his left. Across the street, the only merchant open for business was the Richfield station with its bright yellow and blue vertical neon sign illuminating the night.

*There's the spot*, he affirmed, catching sight of a bus stop adjacent to Thrifty's Drug Store and Woolworths at the far end of the outlet, with a telephone kiosk sandwiched between the two buildings.

"Over by Thrifty's," he blurted, pointing to the darkened storefront. "That's where you can drop us off."

When Loren didn't respond, Steve noticed lines of tension ripple over the man's chiseled face and wondered if he, too, felt the same sense of impending doom. Or perhaps it was something else?

They proceeded through the intersection and hung a left into the shopping center, then zigzagged around an obstacle course of concrete parking chocks and eventually glided to a stop curbside.

Loren shut the engine down, and after a moment of unsettling silence, turned in his seat and stared at the Chosen One.

"My life's been so worthless. I realized it when I heard you say you'd sacrifice everything for your little buddy," he whined. "Perhaps in my next life, I'll be a concert pianist or a successful artist..." then he stopped short, and his eyes flashed, "...once I complete the Becoming of One."

Steve ignored the nonsense. *It's time to die asshole*, he wanted to shout but held his temper in check. "Whatever you say," he replied. "Now help me get Rick to the bench."

Scowling, Loren opened the door and got out, but not before furtively snatching the vice grips from under the seat and tucking them into his hip pocket.

With Loren gone, Steve gave Rick a gentle nudge.

"If you can hear me, we're going to move you next to the pay phones so I'll be

able to call the cops and keep an eye on
you. Then I'm going to kill the
motherfucker," he added matter-of-factly.

Not waiting for a response, he snatched
one of the blood-stained blankets from the
back before sliding out, and gingerly tucked
the gun in his waistband.

Clad only in jeans and nothing else,
the damp concrete under Steve's feet sent
shivers racing down his arms.

By the time he reached the curb, Loren
had already scooped up Rick, cradling him as
if he were an infant, and then purposely
dropped him onto the metal bench like a sack
of potatoes.

THUMP!

Rick shrieked, and more blood bubbled
from the corner of his mouth, dripping onto
the pavement beneath him.

Frantic, Steve carefully covered Rick's
body with the blanket, and when he glanced
back over his shoulder, the monster had
vanished....

# CHAPTER 20

### REDEMPTION

STEVE'S HEART POUNDED. He spun toward the Chevy and the fine hairs on the back of his neck bristled – the man was nowhere to be found. *Where the hell is he?*

Drawing in a deep breath, he did a methodical three-sixty, purposely taking his time to scan the shadowed nooks and crannies of the storefronts.

*There!* A glimmer of movement caught his attention. Out the corner of his eye, he spotted a figure in the darkness, leaning with his back against the wall of an alcove not far from the bank of phones. *What's he doing in there?*

With a lump in his throat, Steve padded toward the man.

Thirty feet. Then twenty feet.

Suddenly, he realized he didn't have money to make phone calls.

Feeling stupid, he cleared his throat, and said, "Uh, do you have any spare change so I can call the cops after you're dead?"

Loren pushed himself away from the wall and swaggered toward Steve, blocking his path.

Less than a dozen feet now separated the two.

Glaring down at the Chosen One with raptor-like eyes, Loren fished a coin from his pants and tossed it high in the air – he wanted to tease the boy a bit longer before implementing his revised plan.

With a cocky upturn of his lip, he said, "Make the call."

"Tails never fails."

Both stared as the quarter rolled in a wide arc and came to rest with the perched eagle face up.

Jaw tight, Steve retrieved the coin and stowed it in his jeans, knowing what was coming next.

"Okay, boy. The fun's over. Take the pistol out and make good on your promise," Loren said while taking a couple of small steps backwards, deeper into the niche between buildings.

"Remember, point the muzzle at my heart and squeeze until all nine shots have been fired."

Steve nodded, then stole a quick peek at the bus stop bench before entering the dark alcove.

UNANSWERED QUESTIONS STILL raced through his head: Did he see the weapon being reloaded? This could be a set-up with him taking the blame for shooting his best friend.

...*More mind games.* It sounded simple enough when he volunteered to shoot the man. The words had flowed out of his mouth impulsively, thinking all the while: *Go ahead and kill the bastard. Why not? Like the fucker said, 'It's real easy.'*

Amid the uncertainty bombarding him, he had to make a choice that would affect him for the rest of his life - the extent of his decision-making at the age of fifteen was what time he needed to wake up and what to wear to school. Never in his wildest dreams did he think he'd be faced having to execute someone.

"Wait a sec. I'll be right back," he blurted before spinning on his heels and darting toward the bus stop bench.

He skidded to a stop at Rick's side. "What should I do?" he puffed, needing reassurance killing the man was righteous.

"Don't..." Rick gurgled, his voice

thick with phlegm. "Saw him put something in ...," then his eyes closed, and his face went slack.

Sick with the horror of watching his pal's life ebb, the moment of truth was upon him. *Quit procrastinating*, Steve reminded himself.

"What the hell are you waiting for?" Loren hollered from afar, stepping out of the shadows. "Get your ass over here and do what you promised!"

Mustering his courage, Steve approached the man, and like a modern-day David facing Goliath, he pulled the .22 from his waistband.

In the stillness of night, he slowly cocked the hammer and heard the ratcheting of the cylinder click into place, recounting what he had planned to do.

The thumping of his heart increased ten-fold as he raised the barrel and paused at Loren's kneecap.

*STOP!* an inner voice shrieked.

Startled by the warning, he altered course and zeroed in on the fiend's crotch. *Time to die*, he affirmed, and his finger tightened over the trigger.

"Tsk, tsk, tsk. That's not my chest,"

Loren said whimsically while wrapping his hand around the vise-grips concealed in his hip pocket.

"I understand what must be going through your head. Hurt him. Make him pay for what he's done. But did you watch me load the revolver, or consider why I handed it to you butt first?"

Stunned, Steve stared at the man, owl eyed.

At that precise moment, the wail of a siren pierced the air, growing louder by the second. They both turned toward the sound, and for an instant, time stood still.

*Fuck!* shouted one of Loren's alter-egos. *It's the cops. Get us the hell out of here!*

In a panic, Loren dashed to the car and switched on the ignition, then rolled down the blood-splattered window to take one last glimpse of the boy who would have been his most prized possession.

The second the engine roared to life, Steve realized he still had the gun. *Holy crap! Fingerprints. What if Rick dies? They'll pin the shit on me!*

Without forethought, he ran to the curb and heaved the .22 through the open window, barely missing the back of Loren's head as the car screeched away.

Speeding through the empty lot, the Chevy's front wheels went airborne after hitting the lip of the driveway apron and sparks flew from the undercarriage when it bottomed out.

Fishtailing wildly across the six-lane artery, Loren quickly gained control of the car, and within seconds disappeared west on Sunset.

Just then, a boxy ambulance with red lights flashing and klaxon blaring blew past the shopping center and turned left toward the entrance of Children's Hospital.

# CHAPTER 21

## THE ROAD SPLITS

THE NIGHTMARE WAS over. Whatever fears Steve had quickly evaporated, yet something in his gut told him he would see Loren again.

With a sigh, he tipped his head and sucked in a deep breath through his nose, much like a dog catching the scent - the air smelled sweet, freshly washed by the rain.

The cold pavement underfoot went unnoticed as he eyed the clusters of billowy white clouds floating against the black sky with a canted crescent moon seemingly smiling down at him.

Grateful to be alive, he relished the moment and smiled back.

*Rick!* Overwhelmed with the feeling of freedom, Steve had forgotten about him.

Shaken, he rushed to his buddy's side only to find him shivering uncontrollably with trickles of blood plopping onto the damp concrete, spreading like coppery veins on a leaf.

"Hurts bad. Make it stop," Rick pleaded in a voice barely above a hoarse whisper.

*Shit. He's worse*, Steve thought as the onset of a panic attack caused his headache to pound away at the base of his skull, muddling his senses.

He had two calls to make: one to the police, the other to his brother. *What should I do first?* he wondered. *I only have Loren's quarter.*

Frazzled, he peered over his shoulder at the Richfield station neon sign, and said, "Hey man, I'll be right back. I need some change to use the phone. Just don't die on me."

Rick raised his head in a feeble attempt to speak but Steve had already bolted.


THE COARSE ASPHALT bit into his soles as Steve sped across the six-lane thoroughfare, forgetting all he had on were Levis and nothing else.

He barged through the door of the service office, only to discover a withered old man with tousled gray hair tilted back on a rickety swivel chair behind the counter, half asleep. He glanced at the name tag embroidered on the grease-stained pinstriped uniform: JERRY.

The startled the attendant jumped to his feet, rheumy eyes agog at the bloodied bare-chested boy, huffing and puffing.

"Oh my Lord, what the hell happened to you!" the shocked man hollered.

My friend and I ... shot ... bus stop...," hooking a thumb toward the retail center. "You need to break this," he gasped, holding up the quarter. "I've got to call the cops and then our parents."

"Dear Jesus! You can use our phone here," the man replied.

"No. I have to go back. My buddy's dying!"

"Why don't you...."

"Listen JERRY," Steve interrupted, emphasizing the name. "We don't have time. Just do as I ask, please," slapping the money on the metal counter-top.

The befuddled man hesitated a beat, then opened the till and retrieved a dime and three nickels.

Steve scooped up the coins and fled out the door after thanking the old-timer.


FOCUSED ON THE phone kiosk while sprinting across Vermont, his peripheral vision caught sight of headlight beams rapidly bearing down on him. Luckily, he dodged out of the way just as the refrigerated produce truck flew by mere inches from him, tires screeching and horn blaring.

With the coins still clutched tightly in his hand, he accelerated and cut through the unlit parking lot while waves of pain crashed through his head with each jolting footstep.

Skidding to a stop at the bench, he fought to catch his breath, ignoring the biting stitch in his side and the sting of road-pebbles embedded in the bottoms of his feet.

Rick lifted his head with a grimace: "Jerry ... gave you hard time," he grunted. "Didn't ... need ... change."

Steve couldn't believe what he heard and did a double take. *How the fuck did he know what was going on in there? I'll have to ask him later.*

"Don't talk anymore. Hang tight and I'll be right back."

Scurrying to the bank of pay phones, he grabbed the first one, inserted the dime and dialed "0".

A female voice came on the line and the

ten-cent piece dropped into the return cup with a tinny clink. He stared at it, suddenly realizing what they were trying to tell him - the call was free.

*Boy am I a dumb shit*, he thought, and smacked the heel of his palm against his brow, exacerbating the throbbing ache hammering the left side of his skull.

Although he was a bundle of nerves, he managed to calmly relay that it was an emergency, and she should notify the police right away. Amid her stammering, he explained they'd been abducted, and his friend had been shot and was bleeding profusely. Not giving the harried lady a chance to respond, he gave her their location and hung up.

*One down, and one to go.*

With a lump in his throat, he put the coin back in the slot and redialed, hoping the same woman wouldn't answer — his next call was long distance and he didn't want to get into a pissing match.

This time when a different woman answered, he said he wanted to make a collect call, and provided her with the number.

On the second ring, Shel picked up the phone and Steve listened anxiously to the ensuing third-party dialog with the operator.

After several audible clicks, his brother came on the line.

"You'd better have a fucking good explanation, asshole! Your mother is..."

"We were kidnapped!" Steve cried out, cutting him short. "I swear to God we got a lift from a psycho hitching home from Sue's," he rattled as emotions rose to the surface. "I already called the cops. Rick's been shot and in real bad shape. I don't know if he'll live."

"Whaaat! Where the hell are you?"

"In front of Thrifty's and Woolworths near Children's Hospital, and..." the distant scream of yet another siren distracted him, and he pulled the receiver from his ear. Craning his neck for a fix on the wail, he prayed it wasn't another ambulance carting someone to the ER.

"Hang on a minute. I hear a bunch of sirens now," he said excitedly. "They're coming closer. Wait a sec...."

Turning from the mouthpiece, he peeked down the road and spotted the flashing red lights of a police cruiser approaching from the east on Sunset.

After crossing the intersection, the

marked car braked hard, and with wheels squealing, swerved into plaza entrance.

A beat later, two more squad cars followed and tore through the vast lot with their side-mounted spotlights converging on Steve as he waved with his freehand to draw their attention.

"Got to go, bro. The Cavalry's here," he blurted. "I'll call you when I can."

"But..."

"Tell mom I'm okay and not to worry."

"Wait! Damn it..."

"Oh. Get in touch with Rick's parents, too," he added before abruptly hanging up.

Shel starred at the handset and a chill ran through him wondering if it was another crazy stunt or if his brother was telling the truth. His stomach churned; how he was going to explain this to his mother and the Shoeman's?

# CHAPTER 22

**THE JOURNEY CONTINUES**

THE FIRST POLICEMAN approached with his service revolver drawn, flashlight focused on the bank of phones.

Squeezing his horrific ordeal into seconds, Steve pointed to Rick, frantically describing in rapid-fire fashion what happened.

The stone-faced cop glanced at the bus stop, holstered his weapon, and rushed to Rick's side while barking orders to arriving fellow officers.

Within minutes, the entire shopping center was transformed into a major crime scene; a sea of blinking red lights and two-way radios squealing with policemen bellowing at one another. Soon, more squad cars arrived, several of them unmarked.

Out of the corner of his eye, Steve spotted an ambulance pulling in from the north.

The blitz of activity caused him to reel, and more adrenaline pumped through him while fielding questions from unknown faces in the crowd.

"Tell us again what the guy looked like," a round-faced man asked.

A plain-clothed detective interrupted: "The boy on the bench. Did you have anything to do with this? What did you do with the gun?"

Another voice chimed in from the shadows, "What's the make and color of the car?"

Then a mousy reporter with an ID tag from the Herald Examiner edged to the front and yelled, "Why are you half-naked, and spell your last name?"

Unnerved, Steve stole a glimpse at Rick being lifted onto a stretcher by two men clad in white and whisked away behind the squall of flashing lights.

Several minutes into the myriad inquiries, a lanky EMT with thinning black hair and a bushy mustache hooked him by the elbow and guided him toward the open rear door of the rescue vehicle.

Liberated from the interrogation frenzy, Steve poked his head inside the cramped confines.

In the harsh fluorescent light, the sight made his jaw drop: amid the mass of

crimson pooled on Rick's gurney, a section
of his scalp lay over an ear as though
splayed by the claw-end of a hammer.

Hot bile burned its way into Steve's
throat. Gagging, he spun around and shot a
stream of vomit onto the pavement, retching
until nothing remained in his gut.

The paramedic quickly pulled him away,
shielding him from the gruesome image of his
partner working feverishly trying to keep
Rick alive.

The mustachioed man then drew a
penlight from his shirt and beamed it over
Steve's brow. "You've got a few nasty gashes
that'll need to be cleaned and stitched up.
You hurt any place else?"

"Aside from a real bad headache,
there's an area on my neck that's pretty
tender."

"Oh yeah. I see it," dabbing away some
of the caked-on blood. "Looks like a
puncture wound."

"Uh-huh. That's where the guy stuck me
with his switchblade."

"Hmm. It'll have to be sutured as
well."

From one of the side-panels, the medic
grabbed a roll of gauze and wrapped it

around Steve's head like a turban, carefully securing it with strips of adhesive.

"Okey dokey, that should do the trick for now. Why don't you sit up front with me while we drive so my co-worker can tend to your pal."

THE BOXY VEHICLE rolled out of the parking lot onto Sunset heading east and then rapidly accelerated.

They flew past Children's Hospital, and Steve followed the neon entrance sign with his eyes: "Why aren't we going there?"

"We're under contract to take all patients to County General."

The answer didn't sit well with Steve, believing getting Rick to the closest hospital was all that mattered.

"Don't worry, kid," said the paramedic, as though reading Steve's thoughts. "They have the best trauma center around and without traffic, we'll be there in minutes."

With siren blaring, the bulky transport pitched and yawed down the boulevard, blasting through stoplights as though they didn't exist.

The blur of darkened storefronts whizzing by had a mesmerizing, almost calming effect on Steve as he gazed out the side window. Then he overheard the man in back shout into a corded microphone: "Patient's bleeding out! Severe respiratory distress. BP 67 over 38 and dropping."

Looking at the road, Steve's eyes welled, fearing time had finally run out for his best friend....

# CHAPTER 23

## OUT OF THE HAZE

IN THE REAR-VIEW mirror, Loren spotted the faint glow of the beacon atop Los Angeles City Hall while fleeing the shopping center. A beat later, flashing red lights heading east on Sunset toward Children's Hospital zipped by.

"Aw shit! It's only an ambulance."

*You should've have started the Becoming of One at the house like we planned*, one of the rabid voices in his head growled. *But no, you decided to toy with the Chosen One. Now we'll have to clean up your stupid mess.*

After roaring out of the parking lot in a panicked fog, Loren's first instinct was to head toward the sanctity of his mother's apartment a mile away – he needed her now more than at any other time in his life, but quickly realized she would never forgive him for what he had done – he cheated on her. All the years of warning him to stay away from women, it was young boys she should have been concerned with.

By the time he cruised past the posh Beverly Hills Hotel and the countless mansions nestled behind tall protective foliage and wrought-iron gates, remnants of night were gradually fading, giving way to dawn.

The open wind-wing drew in cool morning air, yet his thoughts remained jumbled. The more he reflected how his scheme backfired, the more agitated he became - his volatile temper rising while the monsters inside wrestled for supremacy.

"That fucking Rick-the-prick screwed up everything," he screamed at the windshield, pounding the heel of his palm against the steering wheel.

"Whenever I got into a meaningful conversation with Steven, the asshole interrupted, spoiling my moment. Son-of-a-bitch! Why couldn't the little cocksucker die?"


TRAFFIC ON SUNSET winding toward Pacific Palisades was sparse and Loren steered the Chevy close to the curb and reduced his speed - he needed to focus on his escape, but the cacophony of malevolent forces persisted, clouding cogent thought.

Amid the chaos assaulting his senses, something troubled him and he couldn't put his finger on it. He wondered if it had to do with the garage. *Did I leave the door ajar?*

He shook off the notion. *That's not it.*

With static running through him as
though a wire had come lose in the
circuitry, distorting reception, images
flickered through his thoughts like an old
Motorola television without rabbit ears.

*I think it had to do with something
Steven said about an easy way out.*

Unsettled, Loren squirmed in his seat
and the forgotten vice grips hidden in his
hip pocket bit into his butt.

"Ouch!" he yelped.

Suddenly his eyes widened, and the
boy's prophetic words flashed to the
surface: *'You need help. Psychiatric help.
In an institution where you'll be safe.
Where your mother and grandmother will
understand'.*

Like a giant wave, everything came
rushing back as he replayed the scene.

# CHAPTER 24

**REALITY PRINCIPLE**

WHIRLING STROBES BOUNCED distorted red images against the shadowed buildings as the ambulance screamed eastbound on Sunset Boulevard.

It didn't take much before the droning wail and rocking motion caused Steve to become glassy-eyed while staring out the side window. Sapped of adrenaline, he gradually drifted off.

At some point the incessant howl abruptly ceased and he awoke foggy-headed, unaware he'd fallen into a deep slumber.

Out of the corner of his eye he observed hospital staffers in green scrubs milling about, waiting for the ambulance to back into a marked stall and shut down.

The passenger door suddenly flew open, and he was greeted by a youthful black man with a wide nose and forty-eight hours of beard growth. With a weary smile, the attendant assisted him to a gurney and off they went into the bowels of USC County General.

Lying on his back with a lumpy pillow propped under his head, Steve gazed at the overhead fluorescent lights and pastel painted walls adorned with turquoise-blue stripping while being jettisoned through countless corridors.

Where's Rick?" he asked.

"Huh? Oh, the other kid? Don't worry; he's probably in X-ray so just try to relax."

They finally came to a stop outside the bustling ER waiting room; a giant shoebox with funky odors, packed with an assortment of people from all walks of life - some with screeching babies in soiled diapers, others hacking and sneezing. Many seemed to be indigents, disheveled loners from deteriorating shelters throughout older sections of downtown Los Angeles.

With precision-like efficiency, the orderly parked the carriage against a nearby wall and locked the wheels in place before disappearing from sight.

Minutes later, an imposing woman with cow eyes, sagging breasts and oversized keister, materialized at Steve's side.

Clad in a starched white uniform with a tiny, pleated hat pinned to a bun hairdo, her curt demeanor put him off from the get-go.

"Stay here," she commanded with a
scowl. "I'll be back to tidy you up after I
take care of another patient," then she spun
around and waddled off like a sated field
mouse.

Time passed slowly.

Bored, Steve focused on the non-stop
chatter from ceiling-mounted speakers,
paging doctors with indistinguishable names,
relaying cryptic messages like: "Code blue,
room six," or "Bounce-back, room eight."

To help take his mind off the
controlled chaos inside the waiting room, he
engaged in people-watching, playing the game
of guessing what brought them to the
behemoth medical facility.

Some strangers trekked by, nonchalantly
glancing at him mid-stride, while others
gaped as they strode past.

Lost in thought, Steve smelled him
before he saw him.

A bearded wino in tattered clothes and
a face ravaged from years of working the
streets, staggered up and leaned in much too
close.

With blood-shot eyes, he burped loudly
and slurred, "Saaay kiddo, what the hell
happened to you?

Steve grimaced and his nostrils flared - the man's breath was repulsive.

"Do you have any spare cash for a thirsty soul?"

In no mood to deal with the odorous mooch, Steve reached in his Levis and handed him all the money he had - the change from Loren's quarter; three nickels and a dime.

The misfit beamed, revealing a mouthful of rotting yellow teeth, and scooped up the coins with a trembling calloused hand.

"God bless," he gushed. "I hope the good Lord watches over you," then the hapless man turned and shuffled off to find another willing victim.

*If the old guy only knew*, Steve mused.


THE MINUTES DRAGGED on and the hatchet-face RN with sagging tits failed to return. Lapsing in and out of isolation, Steve hoped his brother and the Shoemans had been notified of their whereabouts.

His thoughts were soon interrupted when he detected the cadence of heavy footsteps. Not the clickity-clack of high heels, nor the squeaky tap-tap-tap of rubber-soled sneakers worn by medical workers. No, it sounded more like the clompity-clomp of steel-tipped work boots striding over the highly polished linoleum hallway.

He cocked his head in the direction of the advancing steps and his spirits rallied - Shel and Howard were closing in as though they were on a mission. But like most others who had passed by, they glanced at him and kept walking.

A shudder ran through Steve as the feelings of guilt and rejection collided, forcing pent-up emotions to the surface.

His lips quivered and he cried out, "Shellllll."

The two hulks stopped in their tracks and turned in unison when they recognized the voice.

Shel rushed to his brother's side.

"Where are you hurt because you're covered in dried blood? You said you were alright."

"Sorry 'bout that. I lied."

"When you called, I thought you might've been bullshitting, but a cop contacted me afterwards and gave me the low-down. Now tell me the truth about what happened."

"Where's the sonofabitch who did this?" Howard growled.

Just as Steve was about to reply, a broad-shouldered man materialized out of nowhere and approached the trio - he looked to be in his mid-forties, nearly as tall as Shel, but dwarfed by Howard.

With wiry salt and pepper hair matching the color of his herringbone sport coat and cheeks layered with spider veins from too many bouts with the bottle, he introduced himself as Detective Bill Jackson from the Hollywood Police Department.

After obligatory handshakes, he fished a small spiral pad from his jacket and read back some of the facts obtained from first responders at the shopping center.

The man asked Steve to fill in the gaps; from the time they were picked by their captor until he sped away from the plaza.

"Take it slow, now," said the officer. "Try not to miss anything. Every detail is important, no matter how insignificant you may think it is."

Steve knew the moment would come when he would have to reveal all the indignities he endured, but with Shel standing beside him, he was hesitant to divulge all the disgusting details.

Embarrassed, he averted eye contact with his brother while being prodded into answering humiliating questions.

"Let me get this straight," said Jackson, reviewing his notes: "You're hitchhiking and catch a ride from a guy driving a black 1957 Chevy. You said his name is Loren, right?

Steve nodded.

"So ... you're about to be let off at Pico and Robertson, and he shoots your buddy riding shotgun using a remote-control device on the back seat. Then he threatens to kill you with a switchblade, slaps cuffs on your wrists, covers you up and takes you to a place in Pasadena where he sexually assaults and beats both of you with vise-grips. And somehow you're able to talk this guy out of killing you?"

"Well yeah, kind of, but I'm not sure if I actually..." Steve replied, his voice trailing off.

The interrogator continued: "...And then he hands you the .22, you said it was a steel-blue nine-shot revolver, and demands you kill him with the gun like some kind of executioner."

Jackson raised his eyes from the notepad and scratched the stubbles on his chin.

"That's the damnedest story I've ever

heard. And I thought I heard them all. Mark my words, kid, you'd make one hell of a salesman when you grow up."

"Thanks. But I didn't kill him. I tossed the gun though the car window before it sped away because I was scared I'd be blamed for everything. My fingerprints were on the taped hand-grip."

The craggy-faced detective peeked over his shoulder furtively, and said, "You should've shot the guy when you had the chance because he might well to do the same thing to other kids before he's captured."

With a nod of understanding, Steve went on to explain why he hadn't thought about the consequences allowing Loren to escape.

"I was actually going to do it ... in a roundabout way ... but I hesitated, and then the sound of a siren approaching frightened the guy and he took off in his car."

The burly officer stopped writing, amazed by the victim's harrowing tale, and his hardened expression seemed to melt like warm candle wax.

"Listen, for a fifteen-year-old you did what you thought was right. And since I wasn't in your shoes, it's easy for me to tell you what you should've done."

Not wanting to be overheard, he inched

closer and spoke softly, "Son, a word of advice: If there's ever a time when your life is on the line ... shoot first. Don't hesitate because your brain will screw you up with *what-if's* while trying to sort things out. I call it the *Reality Principle*."

Replaying the scene of the Chevy edging toward the street, the image of black numerals on the front porch suddenly popped into Steve's head: *2014*.

"Wait a sec," he interrupted, raising himself with an elbow. "I remember something else: the address."

"2014 Fair Oaks! The house is white with peeled wood siding, and the driveway is on the left from the street with a narrow strip of grass in the middle all the way back to a humongous, detached garage."

Jackson chuckled, pulled out his notebook and inserted the additional information.

"Nice work, son. You'd probably do well in law enforcement if you set your mind to it and stay out of trouble."

After stowing his pen, he said another investigator by the name of Lieutenant Charles Crumley from the Hollywood Division would be in touch, and then he shook hands and strode away.

Steve watched the lawman lumber off to parts unknown, then peered up at his brother sheepishly, hoping to be forgiven for breaking curfew and sneaking out of the house.

Shel's face was flushed with anger.

Interrupting the tense moment, an attractive nurse with deep-set hazel eyes and flaxen hair walked up to them.

"It's time to clean up this boy so he doesn't scare everybody," she said lightheartedly.

As she unlocked the wheels of the cumbersome gurney and moved it away from the wall, Steve caught the tail-end of the hushed conversation between Howard and his brother.

"...We've got to find that queer motherfucker before the cops get to him. Do you remember the street number?"

# CHAPTER 25

**RESOLUTION**

THE BREEZE THROUGH the wind-wing had helped to revive him as everything came rushing back - how the Chosen One had provided a viable option as a way out of his dilemma.

Loren had to hand it to the boy; turning himself in to the cops was the wisest thing to do. With the right Public Defender and ensuing psychiatric evaluations, the courts would declare him criminally insane, a perfect way to gain forgiveness from his mother and Annie.

In the safe environment of a state-run institution, he could work the legal system, and within a year or so be released back into society to go hunting once again. The only stumbling block would be manipulating court-appointed psychiatrists, convincing them and the presiding judge they were dealing with a lunatic.

*Let all of us take control and we'll make sure you're sent to the funny farm*, howled the voices in his head.

A corner of Loren's mouth lifted. *The*

*next time I meet up with Steven, I'll thank him for the suggestion ... up close and personal.*

Before he reached the entrance to Will Rogers State Park, Loren hung an abrupt U-turn across Sunset sped back toward Pasadena.


THE EARLY MORNING sun poked through the layers of clouds and majestic rays dotted the San Gabriel Mountains like a fine watercolor painting.

The drive cross-town was uneventful, affording him ample time to work through the details of his new plan.

His lips tightened when he flashed back to the torrential deluge from the night before — a bad omen from the start. At the time, he thought finding two boys during a freak downpour had been his good fortune. How wrong he was. He'd have to be more patient in the future.

An hour later, he rolled up to the tri-level complex at 207 N. Garfield. With its colonial-style architecture, red tile roof and white-washed exterior, the building resembled anything but a police station.

Inside the nearly deserted parking lot, he nosed the Chevy to a space reserved for visitors and killed the engine.

With hands draped over the steering wheel, he drew in a deep breath and closed his eyes, contemplating the task he was about to undertake.

A pang of anxiety rippled through his gut - not because of the heinous crimes he committed; there was nothing wrong with that. He dreaded the thought of his mother knowing the dark secret kept hidden for so many years, and how it would all be presented during the sanity hearing.

The image of his grandmother suddenly popped into his head, seated in the courtroom, her withered face lined with pain and disgrace. It was almost too much for him to bear.

Suddenly an adage she frequently used came to mind: *Choose wisely young man. The choices may appear simple, but the consequences can last forever.*

# CHAPTER 26

### BRAVO! LOREN

THE CLOCK ON the dashboard displayed 7:00 a.m. as Loren exited his vehicle and made his way across the asphalt parking lot.

In front of the building, he paused at towering flagpole with the U.S. and California state flags fluttering in the morning breeze.

A lump formed in his throat.

Filled with trepidation, uncertain he could summons the inner beasts, he continued his way toward the arched colonnades of the Pasadena Police complex and nudged open the heavy entry door with a shoulder.

The entrance lobby festooned with memorial pictures and award plaques were of little concern to him as he strode toward the intake counter and the man-in-blue sitting behind a desk.

The officer's weathered face was deeply etched with history, and the plastic identification plate affixed to the glass partition bore the name: SGT. R. ASHLOCK.

As Loren cautiously approached the man, his vocal cords suddenly constricted - his mouth moved but no sound came out. Tiny beads of sweat quickly formed on his upper lip while fighting back the mounting panic.

The sergeant eyeballed the nervous stranger, glancing at his attire splattered with what appeared to be blood stains.

Nonchalantly, as though carrying out a mundane task, he reached for the phone and punched in an extension.

In seconds, a muscular cop with a high and tight haircut and clean-shaven sculpted face materialized through a side door.

Taken off-guard by the striking hulk, Loren stepped back in retreat.

"Hold on mister," said the beefy policeman, grabbing him by the arm with an iron grip. "What's the hurry, pal?"

Loren sucked in a deep breath when one of the malevolent forces from within gained control, and he turned to face the imposing behemoth.

"Ain't going nowhere, Clyde" he replied arrogantly. "See, I kidnapped two kids and beat the living snot out of 'em before raping them. The one I shot is probably dead by now, at least I hope so. What do you think of that?"

The big man's brow furrowed, and in one swift move he spun Loren around and slammed him hard against the wall: "Shut the hell up or I'll button your lip."

After a thorough frisking, finding nothing but a set of car keys and a single .22 caliber bullet, he pinned Loren's arms from behind and slapped on a pair of cuffs, then led him by the elbow to an isolated detainment room.

The stark holding area contained a table bolted to the floor and two solid wood armchairs.

Once the door closed with a metallic clunk, Loren thought, *Step One accomplished. Now for a little rest and relaxation.*

As he eased back in the chair, the handcuffs bit into his skin, leaving him to wonder if they had been as uncomfortable for Steven as they were for him.

"The Chosen One," he murmured with an evil smile.

*The Becoming of One will happen*, an alter-ego whispered. *We told you we'd get through this. The stage is set so here's what we're going to do next....*

THE MINUTES FELT like hours as Loren waited for the onslaught of intense grilling.

Bored, he scanned the sterile room on the hunt for concealed cameras – he had read in a Popular Science magazine some jailhouses throughout the country secretly deployed them in their interrogation rooms.

Nonchalantly, he gazed up at the network of square asbestos ceiling tiles, each containing a hundred or so quarter-inch round holes.

A small section in one of the corners had a brownish stain as though there might have been a water leak at some point in time. Paranoid, Loren suspected a hidden lens was behind the array of dots until one of the circles darted away.

*It's only a fly, stupid.*

Still as a statue, he followed the pesky nuisance with his eyes until it disappeared. In the soundproof surroundings, he could hear the incessant buzzing behind his head and began humming in the same pitch, trying to match the fly's irritating drone.

CLICK.

The distinct sound of the security door unlatching startled him, and his heart raced with anticipation.

253

A heavy-set man in a rumpled dark-blue suit entered the room, legal-size writing pad in hand. With a wiry white mustache and built like a bulldog, barrel-chested and stump for a neck, he introduced himself as Lieutenant Norman Shaffer.

The portly lawman squeezed his frame into the chair and took his time extracting a ball-point pen from his coat - he'd been warned what to expect from the wacko in Room #2 and eyed him guardedly.

Just as he was about to ask his first question, the handsome detainee clad in a powder-blue denim jacket and bloodstained matching pants, blurted, "Some motherfucker hypnotized me, stole my plans, and his crazy friends told me what to do."

The seasoned investigator scooted his chair close to the table and began taking notes while the lunatic across from him blathered non-stop for nearly fifteen minutes.

"So that I can cross all the T's and dot the I's...," interrupted Shaffer, "You picked up the boys at Olympic and Robertson in Beverly Hills and shot one of them with a remote-controlled device you designed. Now tell me again about the gun case. Where is it now but go a little slower this time."

With eyes bulging wide, Loren said, "It's ... in ... my ... car... in ... your

... fucking ... parking ... lot. Is that slow enough?"

The detective lifted his head and stared at the raving madman grinning like a Cheshire cat.

Even though he'd seen just about every degenerate dirt-bag in his twenty-five years of service, he wasn't quite sure if he was dealing with a psychotic killer or a nut-job seeking ten minutes of media fame.

*Time to put the cocksucker to the test*, he thought, and rested his elbows atop the table, clasping his hands together with fingers interlaced.

"Do you know what happens in prison to guys who molest children, or worse yet, kill them?" he sneered. "Well Mr. Smart-ass?"

"Listen old man, I'm done answering questions," Loren retorted belligerently. "I'll talk some more when I'm ready, so this interview is over. End of story."

"Alright, prick. Have things your way," said Shaffer while raising himself out of the chair. "I've got a couple of calls to make."

At the doorway, he stopped mid-stride and said over his shoulder, "If I were you, I'd think twice about jail-time and how child killers are treated by hard-core inmates. It ain't a pretty sight, faggot. You better get used to shitting jiz 'cause it'll be weeks before your butt heals and you can take a dump without screaming."

With a derisive snort, Loren blustered, "I'm not a queer!" Then he tilted his head up and began howling like a coyote baying at the moon: "Yip, yip, yip. Ah-ooooo. Ah-ooooo. Ah-ooooo."

*Now that's what we're talking about,* shouted the virulent inner beasts. *Bravo! Loren. Bravo!*

Shaffer's jaw dropped, and he left the room thinking he'd previously seen it all.

Concerned about jurisdictional issues regarding the suspect, he returned to his cluttered cubical and phoned his old friend, Charles Crumley at Hollywood Division, Homicide Detail.

# CHAPTER 27

## PASSING THE BUCK

A LITTLE AFTER six in the morning, Lieutenant Charles Crumley completed his final report on a run-of-the-mill homicide of a sixteen-year-old Mexican prostitute, hacked to death by her dirt-bag black pimp with a mile long rap sheet.

After pulling a twelve-hour shift, he desperately needed some sleep to rejuvenate.

Ready to call it quits for the day, the telephone rang, and he begrudgingly took the call regarding the abduction and shooting of two kids. The only info available was their names, ages, and sparse details furnished by one of the victims at the scene. Both had been transported to USC County General, one of them listed in critical condition, barely clinging to life.

Resigned to handling the case, he dispatched one of his more experienced detectives, Bill Jackson, to the hospital to investigate. In the meantime, Crumley obtained the phone numbers of the victim's families and contacted them, making them aware of what happened and where the boys had been taken.

An hour later, his extension buzzed and he answered thinking it was Jackson checking in. Much to his surprise, it turned out to be the weathered voice of his long-time friend from the Pasadena Precinct, Norm Shaffer.

After a few pleasantries, his ex-partner expressed the purpose of the call.

"Shit," said Crumley, who proceeded to furnish his mentor information regarding the kidnapping and attempted murder.

"I think you've got the same asshole we're looking for."

"Yep. Sounds like this is your perp," said the aged lawman. "The freak is really whacked out ... or pretending to be," and then he shared the results of his lengthy interview.

"You might be getting a bit too soft," Crumley teased. "The guy I once worked with would've buried a fist in the arrogant prick's gut. And not just once."

"Yeah, well ... guess I must be a little mushy, living here in San Marino with all the snooty rich folk. In the old days, the wise guy would've had an unfortunate accident, like falling down a flight of stairs face-first."

He paused in reflection, and said with

a derisive snort, "Times are-a-changing, Chuck. No thanks to the ACLU, trying to make life warm and fuzzy for societal miscreants and miserable for law-abiding citizens."

"A-men Brother!" Crumley roared. "Ever since they put out a vendetta against decent citizens who believe in morality and the Rule of Law, seems like the fun's been taken out of our job, eh, boy-o? Now we've got to make nice-nice with scum of the earth and the stinking bleeding-heart judges who protect them."

"Can't argue with you there, my friend. That's why the missus convinced me to move away from the dicey *Hollywood* crowd."

"I hear you. But if you recall, the last person who tried to clean out the nest of Commie subversives in the entertainment industry got his political nuts handed to him on a platter."

"Senator McCarthy was truly an honorable man that loved our country."

"He sure was. Screw the ACLU!"

Shaffer listened to his buddy rant on, recalling why he liked him so much. "You always did have a pleasant way of expressing yourself."

"With age comes experienced knowledge," joked Crumley. "But hey, not to change the subject, why don't you ship Mr. Loony-tunes over here? Since this is Hollywierd ... land of flaming fruits, perverts, and troves of degenerates, he'll fit right in.

Shaffer let out a loud guffaw into the receiver.

"Besides, our new captain kind of turns his head the other way so we can do our jobs to keep the city a little safer. Not like you sissy prima donnas in Pasadena, sitting around holding your wee-wee's in a circle-jerk, singing Kumbaya."

"Yeah. Yeah. Yeah," his ex-partner replied sarcastically. "Seriously though, if you want to take a stab at the guy, no skin off my ass since it's your jurisdiction. Look, I'll get the paperwork started and transport the creep over sometime later this afternoon."

"Groovy. I'm going home for some shut eye and be back by three. I'll keep you posted after Weil and I get done tag-teaming the bastard."

FIVE HOURS LATER, Loren was escorted out of the stationhouse cuffed from behind, led by Shaffer and two uniformed cops.

He stopped when he spotted his vehicle on the far side of the lot and shouted excitedly, gesturing with his head, "There's my car! Go check it out. I guarantee, you won't believe your freaking eyes."

The stoic lawman glanced at his prisoner warily, wondering what bombshell he might find.

It didn't take long.

The stench hit him like a ton of bricks when he opened the car door.

"Holy sweet Jesus and Mary!" he yelled, taking a half-step back. He quickly pulled a crumpled white handkerchief from his pocket and covered his nose, holding back the urge to hurl - it was one of the bloodiest crime scenes he'd ever seen and stank of a special malevolence.

Flashlight in hand, he inspected the interior and flipped the drivers-side front seat forward for a closer view of the vanity case.

In an instant, his eyes went flinty when he spotted the steel-blue revolver with taped grip on the rear floorboard. According to the suspect's confession, the boy referred to as the Chosen One had it last.

Carefully, he removed the gun with his kerchief and set it on the hood, then asked one of the assisting officers to clear the weapon and process it as evidence.

*What the hell?* Loren thought. *How did it wind up in the backseat? I'll have to ask Steven when I see him again.*

"One of you men needs to jump on transporting the car," said Shaffer, "because *pretty-boy* here is going to be a star in Hollywood!"

With a mischievous smirk, he turned to the other cop and said, "Make sure the windows stay rolled up tight. I want Crumley to have a real good whiff when he unseals the doors."

# CHAPTER 28

## THE INTERROGATION

IN THE BACK of the squad car, Loren let his mind wander, euphoric since empowering the beasts to manage his actions.

Upon his arrival at the Hollywood Division Complex, a wiry policeman with a jagged scar across his right cheek guided him to an interrogation room.

After a few minutes of nervous pacing, Loren took a seat, anticipating a barrage of questioning from another donut-munching old-timer much like the one he encountered in Pasadena.

Slouched in the chair, he spotted a small camera perched against one of the walls and sensed the presence of eyes.

*SHOWTIME!* a voice in his head barked.

Moments later, a couple of men in starched short-sleeve white shirts and black ties walked in the room; one tall and youthfully muscular; the other in his late fifties, sporting thick wire-rimmed bifocals and a notable receding hairline.

The younger of the two had a ruggedly handsome face framed with wavy dark-brown hair and eyes to match. The man introduced himself as Inspector John Weil, and hooked a thumb toward his counterpart, identifying him as Lieutenant Charles Crumley.

Weil snatched a chair and sat down facing his detainee while his aloof partner stood off to the side casually cleaning his glasses with a wad of Kleenex.

Quickly sizing up the duo, Loren noticed the deep creases around the older man's pale-blue eyes - they bore into him much like his mother's, as though probing the depths of his soul. *Be careful around this guy*, a voice in his head urged. *He wants to hurt you.*

The youthful policeman stretched out his arms and then clasped his hands behind his head with fingers interlaced, stifling a yawn as though conducting another boring inquiry.

"So ... do you understand why you're here at this facility?" he asked.

"Yeah. Some kind of jurisdictional thing."

"Do you remember giving your statement to a Detective Shaffer in Pasadena?"

With a grin, displaying a perfect set

of pearly-white teeth, Loren nodded.

"Is something funny, mister?" Crumley said with a scowl. "From what I've read, you shouldn't be taking this too lightly."

Deadpan, Loren replied, "Every person has a pre-determined path. Mine was to kill a couple of boys. Now I ask, is there anything wrong with that?"

In a test of wills, the stoic investigator glared hard at the defiant man, trying not to show the disdain roiling in his gut.

"Uh, Mr. Neestrom..." Weil interrupted hurriedly, "We're here to help and need to find out everything you did. All we're asking for is a little cooperation."

*Ahh. Good cop. Bad cop*, said one of Loren's malevolent inner-voices. *Alright, let's push some buttons.*

"Listen up. You got my car, my gun, and my addresses. Now go do your fucking jobs and leave me alone. I'm tired," Loren challenged, and turned away in a huff.

The detectives eyeballed each other, then Weil gave the high sign with a dip of his head, and they left the room without a word.

Once the door latched behind them, he

said, "Wait 'til we have what we need then we'll do a number on the sonofabitch in the stairwell. The motherfucker's going to wish he never turned himself in."


THE CRIME SCENE UNIT was dispatched to the Fair Oaks address at the same time the '57 Chevy was being shipped to the forensics garage in Hollywood.

Several hours later, the sealed vehicle arrived at the guarded barbed-wire facilities near the precinct building.

Crumley walked around the car twice, taking his time, then opened the drivers sealed door and stuck his head inside.

"Ah, shit!"

With nostrils flaring, he yelled over his shoulder, "Shaffer got me! It's really ripe in here. Lots of blood," he said. "Lots of blood."

After backing out to let Weil take a peek, one of the CSI technicians pulled him to the side and showed him a white tee-shirt found wadded next to the spare tire. He said it probably belonged to a male child between ten and eleven-years-old and referred to the dark splotches on the front. They appeared to be consistent with blood trace but would know more after lab testing.

The savvy detectives were aware of two unsolved cases of missing boys in the vicinity of Loren's stomping grounds; one concerned an eight-year-old last seen on March 23, 1960 walking down a dirt trail in Arroyo Seco Canyon. The other, age nine, disappeared in July of the same year from the Angeles Crest YMCA summer camp.

The circumstances surrounding the second boy piqued their interest - information they gleaned from unsolved case revealed the child was hiking alone near Neestom's proposed burial site.


IN THE HOLDING cell, Loren seized the opportunity to catch up on much needed shuteye.

Unaware how long he'd been asleep, he awoke revitalized with his crazed alter-egos eager to perform.

Sometime later, a hefty guard came in and ushered him to another nondescript windowless room. Shackled from the front, Loren took a seat, and once the officer left, scooted his chair close to the bolted-down table.

The minutes dribbled by and he anxiously drummed his fingertips on the desktop. Slowly at first, his nails clicked against the metal surface. Then, as though he were Rachmaninoff playing his Third

Concerto, he tapped faster while his head bobbed in time to the imaginary keystrokes.

UPON THEIR RETURN from the impound complex, Crumley was handed two electronic transmissions; one was concerning Shaffer's interview notes, and the other from Bill Jackson describing his conversation with one of the victims, along with the medical summary of the attending physician at USC General.

Crumley's stomach churned after dissecting the reports, sickened by what took place inside Neestrom's car. He quickly shared the info with Weil, and together they strode to the detention area with a newfound purpose.

When they walked into the soundproof room, their eyes widened at the sight of Loren humming to himself while pounding away on the tabletop like a madman.

"I hate interrupting your performance, Maestro," Crumley shouted, "but we have much to talk about."

Loren paid no attention to the snarky comment and kept rat-a-tap-tapping as he reached the movement's tricky crescendo.

The surly lawman closed in and kicked the empty chair, sending it careening into the wall with a loud bang.

"Hey, I'm talking to you, asshole!" he yelled while removing his spectacles, ready to take matters to a new level.

The tapping ceased.

"Oh my! If it isn't Charlie Chan and his Number One son," Loren said with a surprised look on his face. "Y'all didn't knock before coming in. How rude!" Then he batted his eyes theatrically and glanced down at the bulge in his crotch.

"Don't you just love Rachmaninoff? His music makes me hard as a rock. Wanna looksee?"

"Sorry, but we're not on your team," Crumley quipped. "Besides, if I recall, you like them real young, don't you?"

"Hmm ... young? I think that's what you said?" Loren answered thoughtfully. "Why, yes! Yes I do. They're so succulent; sweet and salty come to mind."

In a flash, Weil grabbed the crook of Crumley's arm just as he was about to throw a haymaker and pushed him to a corner of the room - they needed answers regarding the children who vanished in the San Gabriel Mountains.

After calming his volatile partner, Weil took a seat and flipped several B&W photos across the table, pointing to one of them with the tip of his pen.

Glancing at the image, Loren made a small tent with his hands over the bridge of his nose.

"He's cute. What's your point?"

"We found a kid's shirt splattered with dried blood in your trunk."

"So?"

"Well, seems a bit odd to find blood-stained clothing stashed in your car. Especially when the size is a hell-of-a-lot smaller than those belonging to the kids you almost killed last night."

*Damn! Rick-the-prick's still alive.* Collecting his thoughts, he responded with a little help from another alter-ego.

"You said it seems a bit odd. What exactly does that mean? A bit odd?"

"What the fuck was it doing there?" Crumley snarled, unable to keep his loathing in check.

Loren ignored the man and stared at the glossy photo again, lowering his eyes momentarily as though recalling a specific event.

*The Becoming of One!* several voices in

his head clamored.

"Well? I asked you a question," Crumley prodded - he really wanted to bury his fist into the arrogant prick's mouth.

"Um ... never saw the shirt before. Maybe one of your people purposely put it there."

"C'mon. You can tell us. "You've done this before, haven't you?"

"Okay. Okay. You got me," Loren chuckled sarcastically. "I sliced and diced the cutie and then ate him for dinner and used his undershirt as a napkin." After a momentary pause, he raised his cuffed hands and said with a smirk, "I'm only kidding! What kind of monster do you take me for?"

"The type who shouldn't be allowed to walk the face of the earth," said Crumley. "By the way, pretty boy, we want you to take a polygraph. Any problem?"

"Lead the way, Sherlock. Me and my guys are ready for you."

**★★★★**

OVER THE YEARS, Loren had compiled critical data on the functionality of lie detector tests. He discovered they were often inadmissible in most judicial proceedings due to examiner or mechanical error.

Confident he could not only manipulate the system but perplex those reviewing the summary printout - he learned all the little tricks, like counting backwards, breathing techniques, and contracting sphincter muscles. All he had to do was tell the truth, sort of. His ace-in-the-hole, let the inner-beasts take over.

In his confession to Shaffer, he revealed everything ... almost. The Becoming of One was personal.

Now he was prepared to repeat the same version, minus a few important details - items that would arise during the numerous hearings; where reality-deprived court-appointed psychiatrists would eventually seal his fate, providing him with a gateway to freedom so he could once again roam the streets in the quest for fulfillment.

**** 

THE DETECTIVES STARED anxiously behind the two-way mirror watching their prisoner's response. To their bewilderment, everything matched the suspect's original admission - it wasn't what they wanted to hear. They had hoped he might have been involved in the disappearances of other children.

When the exam concluded, the eval-tech explained that the results proved to be inconclusive in a trial.

Regardless of the discouraging outcome, the detectives believed their case was air-tight and their prisoner would be put behind bars for decades where he would be treated fittingly by violent cellmates, passed around like a piece of meat.

Later that same afternoon Loren was escorted to a private intake room where a diminutive stranger with black lifeless eyes and a hooknose resembling a hawk's beak greeted him at the doorway.

In a tone as irritating as a crow's screech, the man introduced himself: "Hello, Mr. Neestrom. I'm Richard Barden, your assigned Counsel. Why don't you sit down? We've much to discuss."

*Aside from the fucking shrill voice that makes you want to slit his throat, I feel good about him*, murmured one of the rabid alter-egos.

*Pay heed to what he has to offer*, uttered another. *Look how his eyes bulge while he's talking. He's a sociopath; a man who believes the ends justifies the means, regardless of right or wrong*.

"Having read the reports," the lawyer continued, "What if can assure you that you'll never see the inside of a prison?"

"Go on, Mr. Barden. But please ... call me Loren."


THE FOLLOWING MORNING, forty-eight-hours after Loren first walked into the Pasadena Police Station, he was transported to Municipal Court for arraignment.

L.A. County District Attorney William B. McKesson charged Loren Rainsford Neestrom with two counts of kidnapping and assault with intent to commit murder.

At the arraignment hearing, presiding magistrate, Thomas Griffith Jr. reviewed the charges and asked Counsel for the defendant's plea.

Public Defender Barden replied, "Not guilty by reason of insanity."

The judge then scheduled a preliminary hearing to be held in Superior Court on October 24, with bail set at $50,000.

Loren had no desire for temporary release, nor did he yearn to see or speak to his mother until the next phase of his plan went into effect.

# CHAPTER 29

## ROAD TO RECOVERY

THREE WEEKS HAD passed since the boys were transported to USC County General.

Inside the private hospital room, the afternoon sun filtered through the slats of the window, casting horizontal shadows across Rick's bed.

A plethora of Get-Well cards were propped side-by-side on a metal linen cart and several flowering bouquets in vases adorned the windowsill, providing a burst of color to the otherwise sterile environment.

There had been a flood of visitors, many leaving behind various mementos like Hot Rod and Popular Mechanics magazines and boxes of See's candies; a special Hallmark card from Melanie sat by itself on the rolling bed tray.

Silently, Steve gazed at his buddy attached to a maze of tubes and monitors, each making its own unique sound - a beep here, a hiss there. He noticed that most of the purplish welts over Rick's face and neck had begun to turn an ugly shade of yellow.

Flashing back to that fateful night inside the ambulance, Steve recalled how he thought Rick was going to die, and the emptiness he felt when they whisked him away to the operating room. He even recollected catching a quick glimpse of himself in the treatment room, not recognizing the battered boy staring back.

Everything about the terrifying incident was seared into his memory: how he later discovered his brother and Howard had raced to the Fair Oaks address, only to find the house surrounded by police; or how disturbed he became after being wheeled to the ICU to visit his pal and seeing Rick's father, Sol Shoeman, sitting in the private waiting room with his head down, weeping for his son.

He remembered it all....


"DON'T LOOK SO sad." Rick mumbled, snapping Steve back to the present.

"Sorry, I didn't mean to wake you. I just walked in," he lied, and pointed a finger at his closest friend's bandaged head: "Love your turban. Might catch on and become a new fad."

"Don't make me laugh. Throat's sore from the trach tube."

"Okay. I'll try and be serious even

though you sound more like Andy Devine on the Buster Brown Show: *Plunk your magic twanger, Froggy. Ribbit. Ribbit.*"

"Blow me," Rick croaked.

"Seems like your hair is growing back," he uttered. "Lucky you have some to cover the gashes. The nurses here keep shaving my head to prevent infections."

"So what if you're looking more like Yul Brenner," Steve replied. "Some chicks dig the bald-look, so quit your bellyaching."

"I'm not bitching, but I saw myself in the mirror yesterday when they were changing the bandages."

"Yeah?"

"One side of my head looks as though they inserted a funky zipper from my crown down to my ear. All I need now are bolts on either side of my neck and a pair of elevator boots and I'll resemble Frankenstein."

"Nice to see you've kept your warped sense of humor. By the way, are they going to cut you lose soon?"

"Depends. This morning the doctor came by and said I might need another operation on my gut."

Steve nodded, as renewed feelings of guilt quickly rose to the surface - his buddy had received the brunt of Loren's fury.

"It'll be the third one," Rick added, then he grimaced while shifting positions. "That bullet sure fucked up my insides."

They both went silent for a moment, and then Rick asked, "What's happening with the trial?"

"Shel hasn't said much, and I don't know what your old man told you, but there's supposed to be a hearing on October 24, and we're not invited.

"You regret not killing Loren at the shopping center?"

"All the time, man. All the time. But I guess things worked out for the best, though, because he's behind bars and he'll probably get the chair for what he did to us."

Rick cracked a smile causing a crease on his chapped lower lip to split apart.

Soon, a trickle of blood oozed down his chin, and Steve quickly grabbed some tissue and gingerly dabbed at it.

"Everyone I've talked to says I should've killed him in the garage instead of waiting," Steve continued. "Almost did, you know, but what the hell ... I'll have to live with the consequences," he said while tossing the bloodied wad of Kleenex into the waste basket with an Elgin Baylor fall-away jump shot.

"Hey, before I forget," he went on, "Did your parents ever show you any of the news clippings?"

"No. Why?"

"Man, we're famous!" Steve said excitedly, pulling folded front pages of newspapers from the back pocket of his jeans. "Here. Check these out."

The first was from the L.A. Examiner. In extra-large, bold-face type, the headline read: WEIRD AUTO GUN TRAP SHOOTS YOUTH.

Then he handed over the second article - the top fold from the L.A. Herald Express: TEENAGERS BARE TERROR RIDE WITH ATTACK SUSPECT.

Rick dropped the papers and looked away. "I don't want to talk about this crap anymore."

Steve stared back. "I didn't realize it still bothered you."

"Well, it does!" Rick snapped. "Whenever I shift my body or have a coughing

fit, I'm reminded. Or when I wake up in the
middle of the night sweating like some farm
animal, I'm reminded. It's like in my head
all the time and I want the shit to go away
... the never-ending nightmares."

# CHAPTER 30

**WORKING THE SYSTEM**

THE DAYS PASSED quickly for Loren, meeting with his lawyer at least once or twice a week.

Over time, he had developed a strong liking toward the strange little man - not in a homosexual way, but as a confidant, divulging information never revealed to anyone, not even Steven.

After many powwows, he realized his alter-egos were exceptionally intuitive concerning their initial appraisal of Mr. Barden - a duplicitous weasel with little conscience - someone he could relate to.

Throughout their private sessions, they outlined procedures and hurdles, working through small details while strategizing possible scenarios. In the end, his fate would play out in the courtroom.

THE PRELIMINARY HEARING convened on October 24, with Leo Aggeler, presiding.

Following lengthy discussions with

attorneys from both sides, the judge appointed Dr. Henry Wegrocki to conduct a full psychiatric evaluation prior to the defendant's next scheduled appearance.

On November 21, the new trial commenced in Department 100 with the Honorable Evelle J. Younger taking his place behind the bench.

Fidgeting with his notepad atop the defense table, Loren furtively eyed the stoic man - he'd been advised Younger served as an FBI agent for many years and was considered a ruthless adjudicator, particularly when it came to cases involving those who preyed on children.

Loren's thoughts were interrupted when the Clerk bellowed the *amended* indictment.

"Loren Rainsford Neestrum, you have been charged with two counts to each of the following:

"Assault with intent to commit murder, a violation of Section 217, Penal Code of California; Kidnapping, a violation of Section 207; Attempt to commit infamous crimes against nature, a violation of Sections 286 and 664; and Assault with a deadly weapon, a violation of Section 245."

When prompted, Barden stood and cleared his throat while buttoning his blue corduroy blazer.

"Mr. Neestrom pleads Not guilty by reason of insanity to all amended charges."

The judge acknowledged the Public Defender with a dip of his head, then opened his binder containing Dr.Wegrocki's report, and said, "Having read the assessment from the assigned psychiatrist, and based on your client's plea, the State, under Section 1027, hereby appoints Drs. George Abe and James McGinnis to re-evaluate Mr. Neestrom to determine Sanity."

"Understood," Barden replied.

"Let it be noted the defendant agrees to additional psychological examinations. This case will reconvene..." Younger paused briefly to review his daily calendar, and said, "...on December 18, at 9:00 a.m. Will that work for you, sir?"

"Yes. Thank you, Your Honor."

Poker-faced, the diminutive attorney with the disturbingly shrill voice returned to his seat.

Loren leaned over and whispered, "Just like you said it'd be."

Barden nodded as he snapped the tabs shut on his leather satchel. From the corner of his mouth murmured, "You'd better be ready for these shrinks. I know of them and believe me they're damn good, especially at sniffing out phonies."

"Don't worry. If all goes well, I'll be out of this hellhole soon. Do your job and I'll do mine."

TWO WEEKS LATER, the Defender's Office received notification that Justice Younger had taken ill and would be replaced with the Honorable Frank Mackin.

This was exceptional news to Barden – he knew the man had earned his Juris Doctor degree in the late 20s from the University of San Francisco and had a close affinity to those in the burgeoning gay community.

At the closed hearing in December, Judge Mackin reviewed the detailed excerpts from all the court-appointed psychiatrists and elected to institute further proceedings under the Welfare and Institutions Code regarding the defendant's Sexual Psychopathy.

A new trial date was set aside for January 15, 1962, at which time both victims would be present to testify.

# CHAPTER 31

**ROAD TO RECOVERY**

ON NOVEMBER 30, 1961, the team of specialists discharged Rick from USC County General - he'd been incapacitated for nearly a month-and-a-half, having had three abdominal surgeries, each with unexpected complications.

While recuperating at home, the days dragged on for Rick, one as boring as the next. Some portions of his shaved scalp had begun to sprout stubbles except for the area surrounding the unsightly quarter-inch wide scar on the left side of his head traversing from the crown down to his ear - the jagged blemish remained raw with dozens of suture marks on either side, a stark reminder of his harrowing ordeal.

Self-conscious regarding his appearance, he had no desire to return to school or even socialize with classmates until the twenty-four gashes were completely covered.

**★★★★**

FRIDAY AFTERNOON, the bells inside Alexander Hamilton High pealed loudly at

2:50 p.m. Teens poured out of their seventh-period classrooms into the streets and scattered like stampeding cattle.

Anxious to visit his convalescing buddy, Steve jogged the mile and a half to Rick's house - he wanted to talk to him face-to-face about the upcoming trial.

The Shoeman's five-year-old Golden Retriever, *Einstein*, welcomed him with his feathery tail whipping back forth, jumping up against the ornate wrought-iron screen door with excitement.

Not bothering to knock, Steve let himself in and dropped to a knee to let the frisky four-legged family member lick his face. In exchange, he massaged the dog's floppy ears, and after a minute of affectionate roughhousing, got up and headed toward the sound of activity in the kitchen.

The scent of freshly baked goods wafted in the air as he strode in the room and he inhaled deeply through his nose once discovering the source of the tantalizing aroma.

Mrs. Shoeman, all five feet of her with tinted jet-black hair teased high in a beehive, was shoveling a batch of Toll House cookies fresh from the oven to a decorative serving plate.

"Yummy!" was all Steve could say.

With taste buds salivating, he reached
in to snatch one of the scrumptious delights
and was promptly met with a playful rap from
a rubber spatula across the top of his
knuckles.

Mindful Steve would do anything for one
of her celebrated sweets, she cajoled: "Want
some? Go get the shlub out of his room."

Then she faltered a moment and bit a
corner of her bottom lip: "He's been real
moody lately, stewing in his room. Go help
him," she pleaded as her eyes welled. "He
needs you."

Steve nodded solemnly, then turned and
padded down the hallway of the Shoeman's
modest California-style cottage, wondering
what he might find.

When he opened the door to a darkened
bedroom, he sighed after spotting the
silhouette of his once high-spirited best
friend on the edge of the bed hunched over
with elbows on his knees and chin propped
between his hands.

Flicking on the overhead light, Steve
walked in and yanked the drawn curtains
apart and then cranked the windows open -
the cluttered room smelled dank and funky,
like a school gymnasium on a hot summer day.

"Why the hell are you sitting in the
dark in your skivvies?" he barked over his

shoulder while gazing out at the backyard filled with arrays of colorful shrubbery and blossoming orange trees.

"I don't feel like being cheery."

"Oh? So you'd rather sit around the house and mope like a spoiled brat, feeling sorry for yourself?"

"Fuck you."

"Now you know why I never went to see a shrink," Steve said, pushing the issue.

"They throw out bullshit advice while most of them are just as screwed up as their patients. And you my depressed friend are living proof."

"Fuck you, again!"

"Listen shmuck, your mom made my favorite cookies and I'm famished, so haul your sorry ass off the bed and put something on. Besides, we've important things to talk about."

Rick's eyes flickered at the mention of food and his dour mood quickly changed. He got up slowly, ignoring the biting stitch in his gut, and threw on his red and black checkered bathrobe just as his mother walked in.

"Sweetie!" she gushed excitedly. "Since

you decided to get off your tukhus, how about a tall glass of ice-cold milk to go with your munchies? Maybe another pain pill, too?"

The corners of Rick's mouth rose.

"And for Stevie-the-mensch, what if I whip you up a *Black and White*? But no medicine for you!"

"Huh? What's a black and white?"

Mrs. Shoeman cocked her head and put her hands on her hips, and with a straight face, said, "You're such a *meshuggenah*!"

Then she cracked a smile and her eyes twinkled: "Vel bubalah, to answer your question," she said in a mock East Coast Yiddish accent, "It's seltzah mixed with a bissel of Bosco and a double scoop of vanilla cream."

Seeing the deer-in-headlights look on Steve's face, she frowned: "Oy vey! You never had one? A nice boychick like you? Vhat a pisher!"

"Oh! Now I understand," he chuckled, grasping her mimicry. "Whatever you want to call it, I'll take one."

Fifteen minutes later, Mrs. Shoeman returned with drinks and a platter of treats, and as she backed out of the room, winked her approval at Steve before shutting the door.

After taking a chug of his chocolate soda and smacking his lips, Steve said, "Guess who got her driver's license yesterday?"

Rick shrugged his shoulders with indifference.

"Sue! And she's coming here tomorrow night with you-know-who."

"Melanie?"

"Surprise, shithead!" Did I make your day or what?"

THE BOYS ATTACKED the warm goodies, wolfing them down while they chatted about school - Rick had missed much of the everyday social activities and needed to be brought up to date on the latest rumors circulating at Hamilton High.

Eventually they got around to discussing their upcoming courtroom appearance.

"So, are you nervous?" Steve asked.

"Heck yeah ... sort of," Rick answered tentatively. "*He's* going to be there, and I don't think I have the balls to look him in the eye. How about you?"

Steve knew Rick didn't like talking about what happened to them, much like his doting mother - she preferred burying the incident as though it never occurred. Things like that didn't happen to nice middle-class Jewish boys. Especially hers.

Of late, every time Steve mentioned the horrific episode, Rick would make some inane joke or hurriedly deflect the conversation to something else. He feared his pal would never be the same, and neither would their once close relationship.

"Hey, I'm as freaked out as you," he replied sympathetically, "but we need to make sure the motherfucker gets strapped to the electric chair."

He paused briefly, and then said with a frown, "You realize the whole thing will be in the newspapers again, and this time all the stuff he did to us will be made public. That's what bothers me the most. People knowing everything."

"Did I say I was afraid?" Rick fired back. He took a couple of gulps of milk and wiped the white mustache from his lip.

"I guess you're right, though, and it ticks me off too," he said, absentmindedly rubbing one of the scabs on the side of his head. "We didn't ask for this shit and now we're going to have to relive it again. I can't even sleep without having freaking nightmares. Rat bastard!"

"You got that right!" said Steve, holding his glass up in a mock-toast.

"Not to change the subject," he continued, "but something's been buzzing around in my head and I keep forgetting to ask you."

"What?"

"Remember when I left you alone at the shopping center bus stop and ran across the street to the gas station?"

"Yeah ... kind of," Rick said hesitantly. "You got in a pissing match with the attendant ... Larry or Harry, or something like that." Then he pursed his lips for a moment as his suppressed memory kicked in. "Nope. It was Jerry!"

"Bingo! My question is how the hell did you know his name and what I was saying to the old fart? I mean, you were dying on the bench a gazillion miles away and I'm like inside the office with the door shut, arguing with the guy."

"Hmm?" Rick murmured, scratching his chin. "I don't know. It wasn't like I could actually *hear* you, but I heard you. Word for word. Don't ask me how. I just did. It was like I was standing right next to you...."

# CHAPTER 32

**DAY OF RECKONING**

THE CONCLUSION OF Loren's Sexual Psychopathy hearing resumed on Monday, January 15, 1962 in Superior Court, Department 100.

The two boys who endured a night of terror sat in the first row, side-by-side behind the polished oak railing separating spectators from the courtroom floor: Shel next to his brother on one end and Sol Shoeman flanking his son on the other. Neither of their mothers had any desire to attend.

Overwhelmed by the backdrop of the chambers and aura of sanctity, Steve and Rick gawked at the hallowed surroundings - the rich wood-paneled walls, the varnished desks, and the pulpit where the judge would sit center stage as though it were an altar to those in the congregation.

Cloaked with their own fears - coming face-to-face with their attacker while taking the stand to relive their horrific ordeal in front of family, reporters, and strangers - they waited anxiously for the proceedings to commence.

Steve rubbernecked the people making their way in, and as he gazed at the tiered section of empty chairs off to his left, he said to Shel, "Hey, what gives? Where's the jury?"

"It's not a *trial* like you think. In a sanity case, a magistrate renders the final decision."

"Oh? Steve replied, not grasping the significance. "You never told me."

"I just found out before we came in because the District Attorney's office never informed us in advance. Now try to relax. Okay?"

THE MINUTE HAND on the large wall clock mechanically clicked into place; it was 9:00 a.m.

"Hear ye, hear ye. All rise," the stoic bailiff announced as Frank Mackin, a narrow-faced man in his late-sixties draped in a black robe made his entrance. Once seated in his high-back leather chair, the people in the gallery took their respective places.

"The State of California versus Loren Rainsford Neestrom," bellowed the bailiff, and then nodded to a uniformed guard stationed in the corner of the room.

The brawny officer silently disappeared

behind a metal side door, unnoticed, and a short time later reappeared with his emaciated prisoner shackled from the front, clad in black slacks and long-sleeve maroon sport shirt.

*He's skinnier and a lot paler*, Steve thought, noticing the remnants of bruising on Loren's face. *Looks like the cops fucked him over good. It couldn't have happened to a nicer guy.*

Escorted down the aisle, Loren glanced at the two familiar men three rows behind the defense table; one ruggedly handsome with dark-brown eyes and wavy hair; the other, much older with a receding hairline and thick wire-rimmed glasses.

He winked in defiance at Detective's Weil and Crumley.

As he was about to take his seat next to his lawyer, he spotted the boys up front. A thin smile crossed his lips: *We'll meet again soon, Steven. You can count on that.*


ASSISTANT DISTRICT ATTORNEY Thomas Finnerty, a slender man in his mid-forties with the panache of a smarmy politician, rose and buttoned the jacket of his grey sharkskin suit matching the color of his hair.

"Your Honor. May I approach?"

The judge skimmed through the prepared brief and suggested both attorneys be included in the side-bar request.

Barden quickly joined in, and after several minutes of muted haggling, the men returned to their respective tables.

From Steve's perspective, the hushed discussions were relegated to a morass of legalese. His first impression ... he didn't trust any of them.

The boys listened attentively as the ADA opened his case with the presentation of facts.

Holding up a document marked EXHIBIT #1, he identified it as Loren's *Project List*, and then read each line on the worn typewritten sheet.

Steve recalled seeing many of the things mentioned on the list and wondered what the purpose was of the other items.

The Prosecutor forged ahead and submitted EXHIBITS #2 through #5: schematic renderings of the '57 Chevy.

One of the blueprints provided a view from the rear quarter panel looking forward. It detailed three characters on the front seat, two of which were far smaller than the driver. Another sketch illustrated a three-dimensional box containing an upside-down handgun with a bicycle brake caliper affixed to the trigger.

Finnerty then proceeded to summarize information garnered from multiple psychiatric reports and Loren's manifesto confiscated from Eleanor Neestrom's apartment.

"Let it be shown the assailant claims to have been abused by his mother as a child and throughout his adolescent years, and that his deviancy morphed into something far more perverted by the age thirteen.

"As a trusted baby-sitter of a neighbor's eight-year-old, he repeatedly molested him, filling his head with abhorrent notions, and over time, taught the child to become his sole possession ... a *love slave*, so to speak. This unnatural bond lasted several years until the boy's family moved to another part of the country. Today, their whereabouts are unknown."

*Aha!* Steve thought. *That's Johnny.*

The ADA pressed on: "By the time the defendant turned seventeen, isolated and lonely without his pubescent partner, his erotic fantasies evolved into a Byzantine world of make believe; one of having a hideaway shared with a youngster who could be nurtured and manipulated into becoming his enslaved lover."

After flipping through a few pages on his yellow notepad, he looked up and said, "According to one of the court-appointed physicians, and I quote, '...as Mr. Neestrom aged, his lust to fulfill his basic human needs appeared to have driven all reason from his above-average intellect.'"

Finnerty glanced at the judge and continued: "With regards to his sociopathic tendencies, all the doctors who examined the defendant implied he may have been devoid of feelings of right or wrong. In truth, the psychiatrists do not have factual data, only supposition. Weasel-words like *appeared* or *may* are not medically definitive but merely positioning jargon necessary to substantiate a predisposed conclusion.

"We contend the accused knew the consequences of his heinous actions because they were well thought out and put into written form; the kidnapping, the physical assault, murder, and even ... *cannibalism*," Finnerty concluded, allowing his last word to resonate.

A hush fell over the room, and people nervously rustled about in their seats, anxious to hear more.

Rick poked Steve in the arm but he ignored the jab, sitting still as a statue, paying attention to what might have been his fate - although he recalled much of the dialog with Loren, many facets of the monster's life remained a mystery. He didn't know if he was now prepared to find out.

"Mr. Neestrom...," said the Prosecutor, pointing a finger at Loren, "...spent considerable time contemplating the difficulty in seducing a child as he had done in the past. As a result, he sought out a pliable preteen, someone in the twelve to thirteen-year-old range just entering puberty. He recognized at that age most boys were susceptible to alternative lifestyles regarding their sexuality and could be easily swayed without much coercion.

"He initially took to cruising the streets of Hollywood and neighboring communities, studying the habits of young boys and where they congregated. He made notes in his journal that most of them resorted to hitchhiking but did so in pairs."

The ADA, seemingly brimming with confidence, produced several police photos of material seized from the house in Pasadena as well as interior shots of the car, including the vanity case positioned on the back seat with the cabling and calipers inside the box.

He showed them to Barden, who barely nodded, and asked they be entered as EXHIBITS #6 through #14.

Back at his table, he retrieved

several articles of tagged evidence and held them up one at a time: the meat saw, switchblade knife, handcuffs, vise-grips, and the bagged .22 set inside the vinyl-covered cosmetic case.

He requested they all be admitted EXHIBITS #15 though #20.

Adding to the drama, he said, "The 1957 Chevrolet Sport Coupe had been rigged as a *death trap*, and to further confirm the defendant's deviousness, the handles to the passenger door and windows were made inoperable as to prevent anyone from escaping once inside the car."

Rick's head popped up and he elbowed Steve several times. "See, I told you I tried to get out after I got shot. Now do you believe me?" he whispered from the corner of his mouth.

Steve nodded absently, mesmerized by the details of deception, as though watching a true-crime story unfold on TV.

"The defendant waited patiently to find the right set of hitchhikers — height, weight and appearance - in order to execute his diabolical plot. A plan that called for shooting the boy riding shotgun, killing him instantly, thereby entrapping his unsuspecting '*love slave*' sandwiched helplessly between them."

The ADA went on to explain in more vivid detail: "Later he would dismember the dead boy with the butcher saw and put the pieces in a military duffle bag and then bury the remains in a remote area of the Mojave Desert."

Steve's lips tightened as the image of Rick shoving him into the car that fateful night, feeling uneasy being forced to sit three-abreast - his intuition had tried to warn him but he was in too big a hurry to pay heed.

*I'll never make that stupid mistake again*, he thought, and turned his attention back to the scene unfolding in the crowded room.

"The interior close-ups of the vehicle..." the ADA said loudly, holding up a dozen or so eight-by-ten black and white pictures, fanning them out like a deck of cards, "...illustrate the ingenious remote-control device designed to fire .22 caliber bullets from a Harrington & Richardson nine-round revolver.

"We can see from the diagram..." he contended, clipping a blueprint to a wooden display easel, "...the man was so cunning, he went so far as to secure a two-by-four block of pine to the dashboard directly in front of his intended victim in the event the projectile passed through the body."

Rick mumbled to Steve, "Remember the wood on the dash? Now we know, huh?"

"There should be no doubt," said Finnerty, "this horrific crime was well thought out; years in the making."

Public Defender Barden shot up from his chair.

"Objection!" he shrieked, his high-pitched voice harsh as a crows caw. "Obsessive-compulsive behavior is a symptom usually associated with schizophrenia. Furthermore, premeditation has yet to be determined."

"Overruled," the judge said flatly. "You may proceed, Counselor."

"Moving forward to the moment when the boy on the passenger seat was shot and presumed dead, the defendant covered both kids under army surplus blankets and drove them to his secret rental house in Pasadena. I hereby submit a copy of the residential lease as Exhibit #21.

"Accepted. Go on," said Mackin.

"There," the ADA continued, "he would imprison his *Chosen One*, as he had come to call him, and within days, dispose the other boy in the manner previously described.

"With that out of the way, the accused

intended to mentally and physically abuse his helpless captive until such time he was of no further value."

After a lengthy pause, Finnerty momentarily locked eyes with Steve, and said, "Mr. Neestrom would then carry out his crowning act: *The Becoming of One*...."

# CHAPTER 33

## THE PLAN UNVEILED

*THE BECOMING OF ONE?* Steve vaguely recalled Loren's words but had sloughed them off as melodramatic gibberish. He held his breath, waiting to see what it all meant.

The single thought gnawing at him for weeks on end, the fact he hadn't killed the man. If he had, he wouldn't be sitting in the courtroom reliving the night of terror.

His daydream was interrupted at the sound of Finnerty clearing his throat.

"Mr. Neestrom was so diabolical, per his confession, he stated that he enjoyed toying with his captive, Steve Bell, the Chosen One.

In the car, he feigned remorse for his heinous deeds and rage-filled beatings, convincing him that he wanted to commit suicide, believing the battered boy would jump at the chance to be the executioner.

"After thoroughly wiping all traces of fingerprints from his gun, he handed it barrel-first to the gullible lad under the pretense it was fully loaded, knowing he had zero experience handling firearms and would never think of checking the cylinder.

"Instead of carrying out the dreadful task in the defendant's garage, the boy insisted they be driven to a mall near Children's Hospital on Sunset and Vermont, knowing it would be closed early Sunday morning."

"Mr. Neestrom agreed, and revised his plan on-the-fly."

The ADA looked down at his notes, and continued: "There at the shopping center, the defendant intended to knock fifteen-year-old Steve unconscious with the vise-grips at the right moment and drag him back to the car and return to the rental house in Pasadena.

"However, before leaving the parking lot, he intended to use the single .22 round stashed in his pocket to shoot the critically wounded Rick Shoeman in the head, killing him once and for all, and then purposely drop the weapon at the scene with the Chosen One's prints on the handgrip.

"Fortunately for the two victims, the sound of an approaching siren caused Mr. Neestrom to panic and flee the shopping center in haste."

Steve's nostrils flared. *That evil motherfucker.*

The State's attorney quickly skimmed through his notebook to a tab containing the initial psychiatric report prepared by Dr. Wegrocki. After thumbing a few pages, he found the typewritten sheet captioned: THE BECOMING OF ONE.

"'...Eventually it would be necessary to do away with my lover,'" said the ADA, reading one of the passages aloud. "His plan, the doctor wrote, said Mr. Neestrom would drug his captive with barbiturates pilfered from his mother's medicine cabinet, and while rendered helpless, eat him slowly, beginning with the penis and testicles, then finish with the tongue and tissue around the mouth."

Without missing a beat, Finnerty added, "The defendant wanted to hear the muffled screams of the boy dying in agony, sacrificing his life in the ultimate act of love - the physical absorption of another human being; the complete fusion of bodies and souls and the cosmic joining of cells and psyches. They would all coalesce, and like a caterpillar undergoing metamorphosis, emerge as a newly formed creation cleansed of his horrible past."

Shel grumbled: "Sure was smart of the prick to give up because Howard and I would've hunted him down and saved the taxpayers some money."

Steve nodded, and replied sheepishly,

"Remember, it was me who suggested he turn himself in."

His brother bristled, and looked away, not wanting to add to the tense drama.

"Once Mr. Neestrom finished his ceremonial ritual..." Finnerty continued, "...he would hack up the remains and put the pieces in a duffel bag, wrap it with chicken wire and encase the mass with a combination of concrete and small rocks, then bury the body at a secluded location off the Angeles Crest Highway. He proudly boasted the faux-boulder would never have been found, well concealed among other granite outcroppings."

Stunned, the full force of the words slammed into Steve as though he'd been slugged by one of Howard's massive fists.

"Eaten alive?" he mumbled to no one in particular.

The ADA then asked Judge Mackin for permission to read excerpts from other summaries prepared by court-appointed psychiatrists.

"Proceed."

The Prosecutor exchanged his folder for a three-ring binder from the desktop and flipped through the sections until he found the index divider labeled: PHYSICIAN REPORTS.

"The following evaluation was written by Dr. J.E. McGinnis, December 1, 1961:

'The accused appears to have schizophrenic psychosis of the paranoid type, thus his bent toward cannibalism. This illness might be chronic in nature. Mr. Neestrom believes he lives in a world of complexities, often controlled by multiple personalities, surfacing as imaginary voices having power over rational thought.

'It is this examiner's opinion his action may have developed directly as a result of his distorted psycho-sexual growth, nevertheless, under the M'Naghton Rule, he was, in fact, legally sane when he committed the alleged offenses, and as defined by the Welfare and Institution Code, he is a major menace to the health and safety of others.' "

Shel leaned over and whispered: "You're one lucky sonofabitch. You know that?"

"Yeah. I am," Steve replied, looking up at the white dome ceiling. "Sure as we're sitting here, there's no doubt in my mind GOD was watching over us."

# CHAPTER 34

## TEST OF WILLS

WELL INTO THE second hour, Steve's name was called.

A sudden rush of adrenaline surged through him, almost taking his breath away.

As if sensing his unease, his brother gave him an encouraging pat on the knee and said, "Give 'em hell."

On his way to the stand, Steve brushed his clammy hands on his pressed khaki pants, not wanting to place a sweaty palm on the Bible.

After being sworn in, he sat down on the heavy oak chair; relieved people couldn't see his legs quaking.

Poker-faced, he eyed the visitors on the other side of the railing, wondering if Loren's family were among them, particularly his mother.

Unable to spot a ringer for Natalie Wood, he shifted his gaze to the stenographer sitting below and off to his left.

With raven-black hair pulled back
into a chignon, she stared up at him from
her triangular pad with fingertips poised,
ready to pounce on cryptic shorthand keys.

The Assistant DA approached the witness
box, and with a fleeting smile - a momentary
curl of his lips - he asked his witness to
cite his name, age, and place of residence.

Apprehensive, Steve leaned forward and
placed his mouth against the microphone
grill, resulting in an ear-shattering squeal
of feedback.

"You don't have to sit that close to
the mike," said the judge as though talking
to a frightened child. "Just sit back and
try to relax. Okay?"

Embarrassed, Steve nodded.

The Prosecutor wasted no time and cut
right to the point: "As best you can, please
recount what took place on the night of
September 16, 1961."

Tentative at the start, Steve provided
details of his ordeal from the time they
left Sue's house up through the moment his
captor commanded him to remove his clothes.

A lump suddenly formed in his throat
and he backed away from the microphone.

When prodded to describe the

specifics of the physical assaults, his fingers squeezed the armrests and he squirmed in his seat - he really didn't want to answer the embarrassing questions in front of countless strangers.

*Breathe*, he told himself. *Go to a happy place*. He couldn't find one.

"We understand this is difficult for you," said Finnerty, "but can you speak a little louder."

Filled with humiliation, a vein of resentment percolated beneath the surface as frightful scenes ran through Steve's head. *Fuck! Will this ever end?*

He cleared the frog in his throat to rein in his emotions, and then glanced at his brother for solace. Shel gave him a reassuring wink in return.

Out of the corner of his eye, he caught a glimpse of Rick, staring blankly into space - Steve never revealed to him all the details he experienced that horrifying night. Now everyone would know.

As the weight of his own guilt bore down on him, he gathered his resolve and raced through his testimony like a thoroughbred galloping toward the finish line.

"Is the man who abducted you here in

the room?" asked Finnerty.

Loren, who had spent most of his time doodling on a yellow notepad, slowly raised his head and his pale-blue eyes gazed intently into Steve's, seemingly locked in ocular combat.

Undaunted, Steve glared back with unbridled contempt, funneling his wrath at the person who changed his life.

With as much animus as he could muster, he pointed his finger at the defense table, and said, "That's the man who kidnapped us and did all those disgusting things. He's a monster who should be put to death because he destroyed our lives."

Loren's face remained passive, but the corners of his mouth rose ever so slightly - it was a Mona Lisa smile - then he lowered his head and surreptitiously scribbled on his legal tablet: BE SEEING YOU SOON, STEVEN.

The ADA hastily intervened: "No more questions, Your Honor."

"Mr. Barden? Cross examine?"

The man with lifeless black eyes and beak of a nose shook his head as though he had no interest in the case whatsoever.

"The witness may step down," said

Makin.

Dismissed from the stand, Steve calmly strode back to his seat, even though he was trembling inside.

"I think you made your point," Shel whispered after his brother sat down. "Relax, kiddo. You did good and I'm proud of you."

A HUSH FELL over the room when the bailiff called the next person to testify.

Rick hobbled his way past the bar, each step noticeably painful. After taking the oath, he gingerly eased himself into the chair, ignoring the intense cramp in his side.

When asked to provide his full name, age, and address, he responded clearly, even spelling out his surname.

"With the Court's permission," said Finnerty, "I would like to read aloud an excerpt from the attending physician's report on the condition of the subject after being admitted to the ER at USC County General."

Judge Mackin: "Proceed."

"'Patient is a fourteen-year-old male Caucasian. Notable evidence he has been severely beaten about the head with extensive lesions and lacerations. X-rays confirm a minor compound fracture with signs of subdural hematoma.

'Ligature marks on the neck. Cutaneous bruising from the mandible to the clavicle. Fingernail gouges and thumb impressions consistent with strangulation.

'Rear-entry gunshot wound resulting in six perforations to the small bowel, two perforations in the colon and inferior pole hematoma of the left kidney.'"

The state's advocate paused a beat, and then remarked, "One depraved man with a heavy-duty wrench and a single .22 caliber bullet caused all that damage to the boy now sitting before us."

Over the next few minutes, Rick fielded a barrage of inquiries from the aggressive ADA until suppressed memories flooded back and his eyes began to well and his voice wavered.

Finnerty asked if he wanted to stop, and thoughtfully offered up a box of Kleenex.

With a resolute shake of his head, Rick dabbed at the wetness with the back of his hand.

"The inside of the car was pitch-black," he went on to say. "So dark you couldn't see anything. One second I'm trying to deal with the unbelievable pain in my gut, and then all of a sudden I'm getting whacked on the head like it would never end."

"Go on."

"Half the time I didn't know if I was wake or like having a horrible nightmare."

"Can you recall anything else?"

"Mostly I was in a fog, drifting in and out of consciousness. I don't know for how long because the next thing I know, my buddy is helping me get my jeans on, saying they were taking me someplace safe."

"At any time were you touched inappropriately or forced to do anything to the defendant?"

Rick jerked back in his seat and his face screwed up in an attempt to mask his deepest fear, the revelation of truth - something he hadn't come to terms with.

"Uh ... like I told you, I kept passing out. Something, um, might've happened," he mumbled, swiping a bead of sweat dribbling down the side of his neck. "All I can remember is that whatever he did to me, it hurt real bad deep inside."

With the boy on the threshold of breaking down, the ADA switched gears and asked if the person who attacked him was in the room.

Shocking everyone, Rick hoisted himself up, and with one hand holding the arm of the chair, he pointed to Loren.

"He's sitting right there. That's the guy who shot me, cracked my head apart, and then tried to choking me to death! He did his damnedest to kill me. But here I am still kicking, and there he sits..." spitting out the words ... "in handcuffs where he belongs. Hopefully, the bastard will be visiting the gas chamber soon."

The judge's expression froze. "Mr. Finnerty! Your..."

Off to the side, Barden discretely elbowed his client, and Loren jumped to his feet.

"I should've killed you in the garage when I had the chance," he yelled. "The only reason you're alive today is because of Steven!"

"The defendant is out of order!" the judge said, pounding his gavel.

During the bedlam, Loren scrambled over the tabletop, but the alert bailiff quickly grabbed him in a headlock, and with help from a deputy, wrestled him to the ground.

Following a brief struggle, they yanked
him up from the floor and dragged him away,
all the while Loren screaming like a madman.

"You should've been dead! The plan was
perfect until you fucked things up. I hate
you!" he bellowed, working himself into a
crazed frenzy before the officers were able
to shove him through the open security door.

Amid the chaos, Mackin continued
barking commands, angrily striking his
mallet against the sound block.

Furious over the disruption, he dabbed
at the perspiration on his forehead with a
handkerchief and stared hard at Barden — he
didn't like the little weasel with the
grating voice and sensed the man
orchestrated his client's outburst.

"Mr. Finnerty," the judge said with a
tinge of sarcasm once order was restored. "I
presume you're done questioning this young
man?"

"Yes, Your Honor."

"The witness is excused."

Rick trudged across the well to his
seat, and as he scooted by Steve, he looked
down and said with a weary smile, "I feel a
lot better now."

On the other side of the room, the Public Defender asked permission to approach the bench.

With a noticeable frown, Mackin reluctantly agreed.

The ADA didn't wait for an invitation and followed suit.

Several minutes passed while the three men argued back and forth. After a much-heated debate, Finnerty spun on his heels and returned to his table knowing his options were limited; the defendant would be found not guilty by reason of insanity or sent to a state-run mental institution.

Before sitting down, Barden unbuttoned his coat and said, "Two psychiatrists were selected at the time the initial plea was entered, including one for re-evaluation. I hereby request two additional doctors be appointed on the issue of Sexual Psychopathy."

The Prosecutor stood, acknowledging defeat, and said, "At this time, the People offer to stipulate so the Court may consider summary reports of all physicians on file.

"We now ask that Loren R. Neestrom be designated a Mentally Disordered Sex Offender and remanded to Atascadero State Hospital for treatment and re-assessment."

Mackin: "Waive further arraignment?"

Finnerty: "Yes, Your Honor."

Barden: "Absolutely."

With three taps of the gavel, the hearing concluded with the accused being declared a Violent Sexual Psychopath.


IT TOOK A few moments for the boys to realize the hearing was over. They gawked at one another in disbelief; each under the misconception kidnapping was a capital offense, carrying with it the death penalty.

Dumbfounded, they trailed Sol and Shel toward the courtroom exit in silence.

To avoid pesky reporters, the foursome hurried down the crowded marbled corridor, two abreast.

While trying to keep pace with the adults, Rick noticed the frown on Steve's face and nudged him with his elbow.

"What's wrong?" he asked.

"For months I've felt guilty for not killing the motherfucker. Now it turns out I couldn't have even if I wanted to."

"So? You're alive."

"That night in the car, before he handed me the gun, it was me who gave him the idea of getting psychiatric help as a way out; a way where his mother and grandmother would forgive him. That sonofabitch!" Steve exclaimed heatedly, shaking his head. "The cocksucker beat the system. He's basically a free man."

Puzzled, Rick scrunched his brow.

"Don't you see?" Steve said. "It was all an act in there. A charade. He wanted everyone to think he was crazy, particularly the fruity judge. After a year or so in the loony bin, Loren will be released once he convinces the shrinks he's cured and can safely function in society. There'll never be a trial and he won't be put in prison for what he did to us. The fucker won!"

"It's over man. Let it go."

"Let it go?" Steve blurted. "From what I heard, the clever prick will be out one day sooner than expected. He knows where we live and what school we go to, and I don't want to have to worry about him showing up one day with another bag of tricks. Do you?"

Rick's jaw dropped as reality set in. "Guess I'll be looking over my shoulder for a long time."

Steve nodded, and said, "You're fucking-A you will. And so will I."

# EPILOGUE

### THE RIDE ENDS

PRESENT DAY

THE STEADY RISE in humidity over the past week had become unbearable for valley-dwelling Arizonans, many anxiously awaiting tropical relief from the sweltering triple-digit summer temperatures. For most, it was long overdue.

On a muggy Saturday in mid-July, fluffy cumulus formations over Phoenix had amassed throughout the day, and by late afternoon, evolved into anvil-shaped thunderheads rising mightily, one atop the next.

Eventually the scorching blaze of the sun gave way and the skies at dusk turned gloomy, masking the ominous volatility from above.

**✶✶✶✶**

OFF CAMELBACK ROAD, the historic open-air Biltmore Shopping Plaza was closing for the night.

Among the people meandering toward the parking lot, a gruff old gent clad in dusty

Lucchese boots, well-worn Wrangler jeans and a blue Ralph Lauren polo shirt, made his way out the south side exit of Saks Fifth Avenue.

With help from his key fob, it didn't take long to find his tricked-out black Jeep Cherokee in the sea of parked cars.

Within minutes, he exited the crowded lot and began his journey away from the hustle and bustle of the burgeoning city.

After passing the recently developed suburb of Kierland, with its array of boutique shops and chic eateries, traffic had thinned while driving up the gradual incline of Scottsdale Road.

Weary and anxious to get home, the man stuck his head out the side window and sniffed in a lungful of air - it smelled sweet, laden with moisture.

Suddenly, a fat raindrop smacked him high on the forehead. Then another. A corner of his mouth rose, and he backed inside knowing what was coming next.

His commute was disrupted when brilliant white shards abruptly lit up the evening sky in a dazzling display of Mother Nature; non-stop bolts of lightning burst through the low-hanging clouds, illuminating them with a spectacular purplish hue while others zigzagged to the ground near the base of the McDowell Mountains.

In an instant, heavy drops careened off the windshield as though someone had turned on a spigot, and the pounding rain bounced feverishly from the blacktop in a ritualistic dance.

The old man flicked the wiper control to MAX and downshifted to a lower gear as the roadway began to quickly flood.

"Oorah!" he hooted gleefully. "The monsoons are here!"

Amid the clamor assaulting the car, a blinding flash struck a metal transmission tower off Dynamite Road not more than a hundred yards away, lighting the cab of the SUV like a high intensity strobe. The sound of the deafening crack startled him, and static electricity made the hair on his arms stand on end.

*Whew, that was close*, he thought, and he grasped the steering wheel tighter.

With his speed cut well below the posted limit, he trekked onward, cautiously dodging rolling tumbleweeds and floating debris along the dark stretch of highway toward his tony estate at the Mirabel Golf Club near Carefree, a small master-planned hamlet of exclusive upscale living.

Minutes later the ghostly aura of

floodlights surrounding the familiar Shell
Station appeared ahead off to his right -
most mornings he would stop in for a cup of
Joe and shoot the breeze with the mechanics
to reminisce about hot rods and the *good old
days*.

As he neared the gas station, his
peripheral vision caught the movement of two
silhouettes standing at the corner with
thumbs in the air, hitchhiking.

A dreadful image popped in his head:
"No frigging way," he mumbled. "Don't even
think about it."

The rugged old-timer nervously raked
his fingertips across his scalp and gently
massaged one of the seven deep scars well-
hidden beneath the clump of wavy salt and
pepper hair. *Some memories will never cease*,
he mused.

The veil of silver toothpicks continued
to pummel the car with ferocity as he closed
in on the red light.

Slowing down for the signal, it became
apparent the hitchhikers were young, waving
their arms helter-skelter, desperately
trying to attract his attention.

*Oh, what the hell, they're just kids*,
he thought, and coasted to a stop alongside
them.

The doors flew open, and the boys with rain-soaked sweatshirts jumped in. The one sitting shotgun slid his drenched hoodie back, revealing a damp mat of stringy dark-red hair.

Surreptitiously, the man sized him up: short and pudgy with a well-rounded pale face, puffy cheeks and a pushed-in nose - the kind of boy who gets bullied at school by cruel classmates.

Before he got a glimpse of the lad seated in back, the interior lights had dimmed, but thought he might've been lanky and dark complexioned.

"Where you all headed?" he asked.

In a pitchy voice akin to someone going through puberty, Pug-nose said, "The Boulders."

"Not a problem. I know the place well and pass it on the way home every day," the man replied, wondering why the youngsters would be going to a Five-Star resort.

The pungent scent of marijuana wafted in the air when the boy in back leaned forward between the bucket seats and slurred, "Who'd thunk a couple of homies like us would get trapped in a fucking storm? Dude, you saved our butts!"

With an edgy smile, the crusty driver

eased the car back onto the desolate road, reconsidering his decision to pick up the boys. *Stop being a worrywart, you old fart*, said an inner voice.

He turned to the kid next to him: "By the way, my name's Steve. What's yours?"

"Frank. And the punk behind you..." hooking a thumb over his shoulder, "..."is Armando, but we just call him *Loco* because of all the crazy stuff he does."

Steve's brow furrowed at the odd moniker but became distracted when another massive bolt illuminated the sky, its vast tentacles spreading over the dark basin like veins on a leaf.

"How old are you?"

"Fourteen. Why?"

"You're the first hitchhikers I ever picked up," the man said, and immediately regretted his words, thinking he probably sounded like a frightened hen.

"Seeing you guys out there in the middle of a monsoon downpour made me think of something terrible that happened to my friend and I when we were about your age."

"Oh yeah? What was it?"

"Well, it's kind of bizarre, and pretty

gruesome."

"Way cooool!" said the wiry boy in back.

With a nod of his head, Steve Bell stared at the road and allowed his mind to momentarily drift - scenes flipped into his head like a Kinetoscope, recalling everything leading up to the fateful night on September 16, 1961. In seconds it all unfolded as though speed-reading his past from a paperback novel.

"Okay. I hope you'll learn something from what I'm about to tell you."

Up the street, the headlight beams lit up a reflective yellow warning sign of an upcoming dip, so he held the wheel firmly before entering the flooded wash.

The car shuddered as silt and water sprayed through the wheel-wells and over the hood while traversing the rushing torrent.

"Back in 1961," he went on, relaxing once the four-wheel drive emerged from the gully, "we were thumbing a ride home one night in the middle of a terrific thunderstorm...."

THE DEBRIS-STREWN highway had become an even greater challenge making their way up the gentle grade as Steve shared snippets of his harrowing tale.

"Wow! That's one heck of a story," said Pug-nose Frank, paying little attention to the hostile conditions outside.

"Whatever happened to your friend?"

More flashbacks filtered into Steve's thoughts, and he went silent for a beat.

"After the hearing, our relationship tapered off," he finally uttered with a tinge of remorse, wishing he could have changed the way things turned out - Rick's ongoing bouts with depression and their heated feud over a girl drove the once best friends apart.

"Rick got drafted into the Army after graduating high school and was shipped off to Vietnam. Luckily, he got sent home six months later on a medical discharge due to issues stemming from the gunshot wound when we were kidnapped."

Reliving his moment-in-time, Steve took in a deep breath and added, "...We sort of went our separate ways after he got out of the military. Socially, our paths didn't cross much but we kind of stayed in touch through the years.

"One day he moved out of the area and we stopped communicating altogether. Several years ago, I heard through the grapevine he died in 2002. He was only fifty-five."

"Gee, you really lucked out, mister."

"Yeah. I'm like a cat with nine lives," Steve chortled. "But at sixty-five, I think they're almost used up."

He didn't bother to mention the fact he had received a mysterious manila packet in 1964 with no return address. Inside the sealed envelope, an 8x10 color photo of an oil painting titled: "The Becoming of One." It was a portrait of a boy who bore a striking resemblance of what he had looked like at age fifteen. The backside had been signed, "Always watching. Love, Laura." Taped to it, a twenty-inch lock of strawberry-blond hair.

THE STOPLIGHT AT Carefree Highway loomed half-a-mile ahead.

Tired of mundane jabbering, Steve wanted to get home to soak in the Jacuzzi and down a few ice-cold bottles of Pacifico while fantasizing about the women throughout his life, playing the mental game of, 'Now what was her name'?

Only another couple of miles up the road, he thought.

From the shadows directly behind him, a voice snapped him out if his daydream.

"So, we're like the first dude's you've ever given a lift to, eh?"

Steve detected a rough edge in Armando's tone but sloughed it off.

"Yeah, you are. I've been reluctant to give rides to strangers, even kids like you. See, when I was growing up there wasn't much violence as compared to today."

What his passengers didn't know, he had learned well from his terrifying experience. Ever since that fateful night, he adopted the Boy Scout motto: *'Be Prepared'*.

Pug-nose chimed in: "Do you really think it's that violent now?"

"Heck yeah!" Steve replied adamantly. "Some of the stories I've seen regarding the behavior of teenagers blows my mind: like playing barbaric Xbox video games twenty-four seven while listening to hard-core rap-crap with crude lyrics about banging little girls or snuffing out cops to make a name for themselves. Hell, nowadays it seems as though young people going to jail is like wearing a stupid badge of honor."

"Man, ain't no big thang," Armando boasted.

"Ohh? Well just look at Hollywood. They pump out movies loaded with blood, guts and gore while the hypocrites who star in them speak out against the use of guns, and then get facetime on nightly news denigrating police officers who try to enforce the law.

"Who cares?" said Frank. "Laws are stupid."

Exasperated over their juvenile ignorance, Steve pressed the issue.

"What about children raised on psychotropic drugs with some winding up mass-murderers because someone hurt their little feelings and they couldn't cope with the pressure and then take it out on innocent people?"

Worked up, forgetting he was talking to naive teens, he blurted, "What the hell's wrong with kids today?"

Instead of responding, Frank said coldly, "You can drop us off over there," pointing with a finger, "and we'll walk the rest of the way."

Steve didn't reply – the duo had worn out their welcome.

As they approached the narrow driveway for the resort's maintenance crew, he guided the Jeep off-road onto a soft mound of muddy grass.

After putting the car in neutral, he chuckled, feeling silly for his long-winded rant, and said, "Sorry if it seemed like I was preaching. I guess I'm too old and don't understand."

"And ju never will, you fuck-ing pendejo," hissed Armando from the back seat, his accent suddenly much more pronounced.

The hackles on Steve's neck bristled as a sense of déjà vu swept through him, and he casually lowered his left arm.

His eyes darted to the rear-view mirror just in time to see the glint from the barrel of a chrome-plated revolver pointed at his head.

BANG! BANG!

This book is a work of fiction based upon
true events. Some of the names, characters,
and dialog are fictitious. Any similarity to
real persons, living or dead, is
coincidental and not intended by the author.

**Copyright © 2008 by Stan Wald**